Encyclopedia of Pet Mice

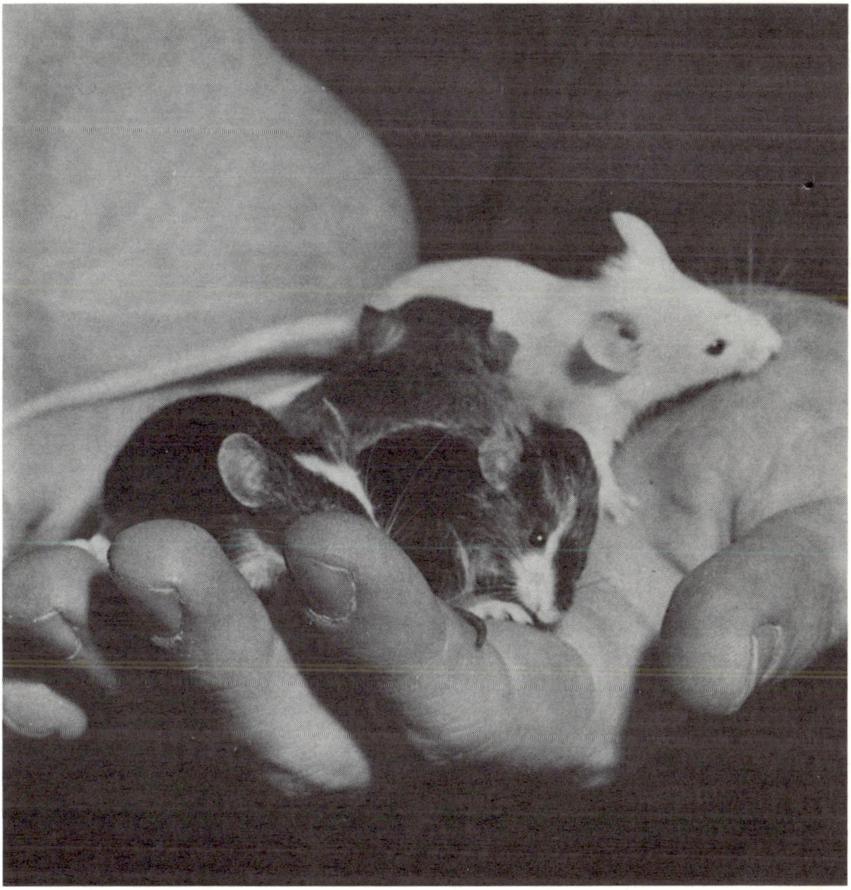

TONY JONES

Frontis: A handful of fancy mice. Photo by A. P. May.

Cover: CLI

ISBN 0-87666-910-0

© 1979 by T.F.H. Publications, Inc.

Distributed in the U.S. by T.F.H. Publications, Inc., 211 West Sylvania Avenue, PO Box 427, Neptune, NJ 07753; in England by T.F.H. (Gt. Britain) Ltd., 13 Nutley Lane, Reigate, Surrey; in Canada to the book store and library trade by Beaverbooks Ltd., 150 Lesmill Road, Don Mills, Ontario M38 2T5, Canada; in Canada to the pet trade by Rolf C. Hagen Ltd., 3225 Sartelon Street, Montreal 382, Quebec; in Southeast Asia by Y.W. Ong, 9 Loring 36 Geylang, Singapore 14; in Australia and the South Pacific by Pet Imports Pty. Ltd., P.O. Box 149, Brookvale 2100, N.S.W. Australia. Published by T.F.H. Publications, Inc., Ltd., The British Crown Colony of Hong Kong.

Contents

PREFACE
1. A SHORT HISTORY OF THE FANCY.......... 9
2. MICE AS PETS.................... 12
3. MAKING A START—INITIAL PURCHASE.... 21
4. HOUSING 26
5. MAKING RACKS AND BREEDING BOXES.... 30
6. BEDDING 42
7. FEEDING........................ 46
8. BREEDING 55
9. FOSTERING 67
10. AILMENTS 69
11. "A DAY AT A SHOW IS A TONIC"........ 72
12. SHOWS—HOW TO ENTER............. 77
13. SHOW PREPARATION.............. 85
14. STEWARDING—MEANS TO AN END...... 93
15. THE STANDARD OF EXCELLENCE....... 97
16. THE SELFS..................... 100
17. TANS......................... 127
18. MARKED...................... 138
19. ANY OTHER VARIETY.............. 166
20. BUILDING UP A STUD............. 202
21. INBREEDING................... 206
22. GENETICS..................... 209
23. EXPERIMENTAL BREEDING......... 211
24. FANCY RATS................... 215
INDEX

To the
Mouse Fancy

Preface

For generations children have kept mice as pets, but few people are aware of the existence of a Mouse Fancy whereby "fanciers" breed and exhibit different varieties of fancy mice in an effort to win prizes at competition shows.

For those who have graduated from the white mouse kept in the trouser pocket, the hobby of mouse-keeping and exhibiting is a serious business. Competition is keen, but is of a healthy nature. Mouse fanciers are friendly people, always ready to help and advise the beginner.

If you are fond of animals and enjoy the excitement of competition, whether you are 6 or 60, the Mouse Fancy may be for you. Outlay is far cheaper than any other livestock hobby; rearing is simple and requires little space. There are over fifty different colors and breeds of fancy mice to choose from: something for every taste!

It is my intention in this book to guide the reader in his transition from the petshop mouse to acquiring, managing and exhibiting top quality fancy show mice.

Quiet pride is reflected in the face of this owner of a prize-winning Long-Haired Mouse.

1: A Short History of the Fancy

In 1895, the Mouse Club was inaugurated when a group of English enthusiasts, led by the late Walter Maxey from London's East End, got together through an interest in keeping and breeding pet mice. Mr. Maxey has rightly been dubbed "Father of the Mouse Fancy."

These fanciers laid down a set of "Rules and Standards of Excellence" that has been changed only little over the course of time. The prime objective is, of course, to promote the breeding and exhibiting of fancy mice. Shows were organized under the patronage of the N.M.C. (National Mouse Club) and trophies were awarded at the important cup shows held over the years. Championships were also awarded those mice attaining the status required of the rules. Officials and judges were elected annually by members' ballots. A special cage was designed by Mr. Maxey and was adopted as the official show cage. It was termed the "Maxey" cage.

Some early breeds were Agoutis (mice with a wild type of coat pattern and color), Cinnamons, Silver Greys, Self Reds, Blacks, Blues and Chocolates, and of course the Albino, which the Fancy calls the Pink-Eyed White. All of these uniquely different colors evolved from the common house mouse *(Mus musculus)*. By selective

9

breeding, fanciers have been perfecting various "sports" or mutants. It can now be said that the acme of perfection has *almost* been attained. One says *almost* because there will always be room for improvement. In short the perfect exhibition animal has never been bred.

Credit must be paid to the past generations of fanciers for persevering and trying to perfect most of our present day varieties. It is indeed remarkable to contrast the wild mouse with its fancy cousin: One might just as well compare a wolf with a Chihuahua.

Mus musculus in nature is a weedy, disease-ridden creature. Its exhibition descendant has an all around clean appearance with shining coat, bright bold eyes, alert ears and an inquisitive expression. Wild mice are small and remarkably unhealthy, yet through years of selection we now have mice as long as 9 to 11 inches in length from the nose to the tip of the tail. These mice are the epitome of health and fitness, with a pleasing freedom from vices or from the tendency to bite or escape.

Over the past 80 years the N.M.C. has become one of the most respected livestock associations. From its base in Great Britain, it has a world-wide membership.

Mr. Walter E. Maxey, the founder of the first mouse club in London. He also designed the official show cage of the club.

2: Mice as Pets

It is probably true to say that the majority of the serious adult mouse fanciers of today kept mice as pets during their younger years. Many white mice pairs bought in a pet shop have begun a lifelong interest and fascination for countless people. It is important for us to fill our leisure hours with some creative activity that is a complete change from our everyday work. There are many such pastimes, for example gardening, reading, handicrafts, social clubs, sports, etc. If your leisure-time leaning is towards breeding animals, and even if you can afford only a little space, time and money, the mouse fancy might well suit you.

Apart from the obvious pleasures of breeding your own strain, there is a tremendous social aspect, for people are brought together from all walks of life through the attraction of one of the smallest domesticated creatures, the fancy mouse.

It is essential that children develop an understanding and appreciation of all forms of animal life. This is especially true in the present age because many types of animal life are becoming critically scarce, in some cases almost extinct. Perhaps the humble mouse will help future generations care more for the natural world around us, for it is strange how a love for animals grows among youngsters who first kept mice as pets. Particularly in schools, this interest can be fostered by the

It does not take too long for a child to realize the fun of having and taking care of a pet. This activity may be temporary in some children but may last longer in others, leading to serious hobby or even a career as a breeder. A Three Lions photo.

efforts of an ambitious teacher. A simple breeding colony can be set up with little trouble using a few old aquariums. Animal habits and social behavior can then be observed and enjoyed by the children under supervision of the teacher. Furthermore, once breeding has started, heredity of both color and form can be studied at length.

Few other animals lend themselves so readily to such study. Indeed, it is well known that the mouse has been the subject of extensive research for the ultimate benefit of mankind. Because of their charming mannerisms, early maturity and prolific habits, the interest of the child will not wane. Something new will always be happening in the colony. A litter may have been born during the night, for instance, and the patient anticipation while waiting for the young to color-up in the nest will be rewarded by days of interest as the young gradually mature.

If you are unable to keep mice at school (although surely you can find an excuse for using them in some practical manner, e.g., a biology class), an accommodation at home for pet mice is very simple and requires only a little space.

Aquariums make good homes. They are easy to keep clean, and the owner can study the antics of his pets with ease. If you are unable to obtain an old aquarium, a similar mouse house can be made out of transparent plastic fish tanks. These are heartily recommended, as they are cheaper than new glass aquariums. I am not in favor of any kind of metal cage. They are cold for mice, they often have a tendency to rust, and they are usually poorly constructed. If you are making your own cage, wood is the best material. Remember, though, that mice are rodents and have a natural tendency to gnaw, so keep watch for possible "Houdinis"! Ready-made aquariums are really best. The important point to remember is that mice will sur-

Plastic cages with appropriate cover and special attachment for drinking bottle are also available commercially. Photo by M.F. Roberts.

A plastic storage box (available in many shops) serves as a breeding box for a Dutch Mouse. After weaning the babies can be transferred to larger living quarters like a regular cage or an aquarium. Photo by A.P. May.

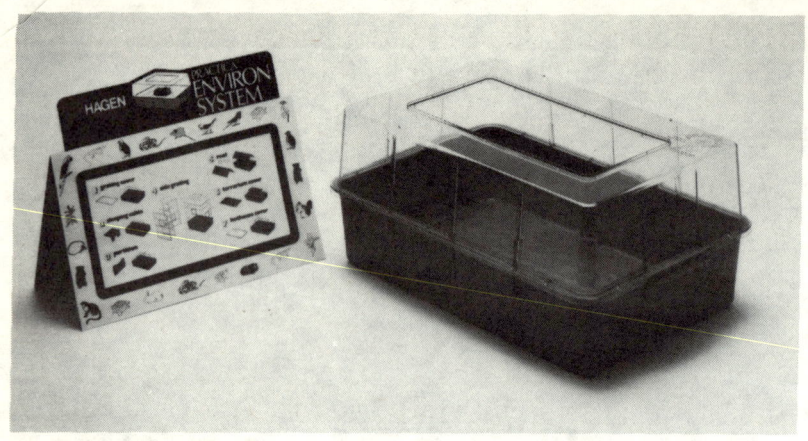

A container designed especially for small mammals and marketed as the Hagen Habitat.

An all-glass aquarium will serve well as a holding cage for mice or other small mammals. The hood and glass cover are easily replaced by a movable wire covering.

vive happily in any shape or form of cage provided it is warm and has ample ventilation.

Once you have a cage, you can prepare for the arrival of its occupants. A layer of fairly coarse cedar shavings about one-half inch deep should be put on the floor of the cage. For bedding, use hay or paper shavings. Never use cotton, wool or any similar bedding, because mice might swallow a little of it; if they do, the intestines will become blocked and the animal will surely die. Detailed information on housing, bedding and feeding is provided in the relevant sections of the book. It is enough to say at this stage that the pet owner should *not* give sweets, chocolates or cheese to mice, as these foods are totally unsuitable. Contrary to popular belief, pet mice do not even appreciate cheese; they prefer seeds or a piece of carrot.

Mice are exceedingly clean little animals and have no odor. Unfortunately, their urine does have a pungent odor, and if the cages are not kept scrupulously clean that infamous "mousey" smell will soon become apparent. The best thing for all pet owners to do is to clean the cage regularly and supply fresh bedding at least once a week. The mice will be healthier, and no one will have an excuse for complaining about your pets.

If the mouse owner looks after his mice well, there is no reason why they should not be kept in the house. A spare room or attic will do nicely, but if necessary a garden shed will do just as well. Mice are hardy creatures and can withstand extreme changes in temperature if housed and fed properly, so the owner need not be concerned about his pets provided he feeds them well every day.

If the owner wishes to breed his mice, I would suggest that he or she start with a trio, that is, a buck (male) and two does (females). If breeding is not intended, it is best to purchase only does. Rodents tend to form family col-

A commercially manufactured cage of clear plastic with a tray, an exercise wheel, a feeding box, and a series of tunnels. Here it is being shown as a home for hamsters, but mice can use it as well. Photo courtesy of Metaframe Corporation.

A typical wire cage for mice fitted with the necessary equipment such as a movable bottom tray, an exercise wheel, a feeding trough, and a water bottle. Photo by L. van der Meid.

onies, and two strange bucks might fight quite savagely. *Do not keep* a mouse by itself, as mice are gregarious creatures and prefer company at all times.

For additional entertainment an exercise wheel can be purchased from your local pet dealer. The mice will soon learn to tread the wheel and will busy themselves for many hours in this way. A chunk of dry, slightly stale bread placed in the cage will soon be investigated, and tunnels will be eaten into the bread overnight. Another easy and inexpensive way of keeping the mice active is to put the cardboard roll from an end of toilet paper into the cage. Then you can see which mouse is brave enough to venture through the roll, until they tear up the cardboard and use it as nesting material. The ingenious owner can invent many other similar games and tricks to keep the pets and himself amused. Your pet shop has many articles for mouse entertainment, but a chew toy is necessary and "Nylabone" is the best chew toy for your mice. Mice are among the easiest pets to maintain properly, and if handled constantly but gently they will become exceedingly tame.

Finally, without meaning to deprecate the value of the pet shop mouse, I'd like to make the relevant point that pedigreed show mice are certainly no more difficult to keep and require basically the same management.

Remember, if you are going to breed mice, the time will come when you will have an excess of stock. Unless you sell some to a person who wants food for his pet owl or snake, your mouse colonies will be overcrowded in a short time. This might cause a health hazard to the mice and will definitely make maintenance more difficult. There is always a demand for top-class show stock, so bear this in mind when you make your initial purchase.

3: Making a Start—Initial Purchase

It is obviously common sense to prepare suitable accommodations before making your initial purchase of fancy mice. However, how many of us are blessed with the virtue of patience? Once the pet owner and animal lover has decided he or she wants to keep something, his enthusiasm demands immediate satisfaction. For this reason I am dealing first with the initial purchase of exhibition stock, although I cannot stress too strongly how important it is to have some type of housing and food available before the "giant step" is taken.

While it is certainly a grave mistake to "put the horse before the cart" and to purchase stock before all else is ready, it is even more dangerous to accept the first offer that comes your way. You may well be purchasing something you don't really want; it may be that a certain variety is too difficult for a novice to begin with. Nothing is so daunting as complete lack of success for the beginner, who often gives up the hobby before giving himself a fair chance.

There is no better way of finding out about the mouse fancy, or any other fancy for that matter, than by actually attending a show, especially if it is one of the larger championship events. Do not be afraid of making yourself known as a newcomer. Go up to the show secretary, who will be the person writing out the prize cards. Explain to him your interest and he will soon introduce you to a fellow fancier who can answer your queries and show you all the different varieties that are on the show bench in the little Maxey cages waiting to be judged. Perhaps you will even be fortunate enough to be introduced to a leading exhibitor of the variety that you wish to make a start with, and hopefully he will be able to set you up with some foundation breeding stock.

If the beginner cannot go to a show to choose his stock, he should contact a pet shop and ask if he could visit a mousery at some convenient time. I am sure the fancier would be only too pleased to show the novice his methods of keeping mice. Many a lifelong friendship has been made from such a meeting. If the particular fan-

This judge is giving an entry a final check prior to recording his evaluation.

Spectators at a mouse show looking over the different mice on display.

cier from whom you wish to purchase stock lives more than a reasonable distance for a visit, then write to ask if he has any stock for sale, explaining that you have just started, but be prepared to wait for good foundation stock. Never forget to enclose a stamped, self-addressed envelope with your letter, as this is the proper thing to do when first corresponding with a senior fancier. Of course, your pet shop might be interested in getting special mice just for you.

Some final words of advice regarding initial purchase for those wishing to succeed in breeding and exhibiting. Do not be tempted to take on more than one, or at most two, varieties to begin with. I know this is difficult because there are so many different colors to attract each individual. If you really must have more than one breed, then choose those that are compatible with each other (examples: Self Fawns and Champagne Tans or Agoutis and Cinnamons). Buy the best available and from one source only. It is not good to acquire a buck from one fancier and does from someone else as there is no way of knowing what the subsequent litters will be. It is always preferable to keep within the family strain if the fancier wishes to breed winners consistently. The process of building a strain is not something that occurs overnight. It is a gradual process of improvement (through each generation) by selection. The winning mice seen at shows did not come about when their parents were chosen and mated by the fancier. No indeed, the very best mice were the results of intensive care and inbreeding or line-breeding within the family. Even the most experienced fanciers take time to build up a stud of mice that bear a resemblance to each other and that are close to the standard of excellence required. These mice are known as a "strain"; that is, they are all of the same bloodline. So how can a novice be expected to achieve good results by cross-breeding? It is almost impossible.

So until he gains experience and wishes to experiment for himself, the novice should purchase his mice from one reliable breeder. If the novice then accommodates and manages well and selects only the best for future matings, success will surely follow. Many a beginner, and that includes boys, girls and adults, has won Best-in-Shows and Championships from the first generation of litters born from good quality stock. Because of the generosity of many experienced fanciers in supplying well-established stock, it is possible for the novice to go right on to the top in a very short time. The mouse fancy is almost unique in this respect.

The author with two of his prized mice.

4: Housing

Accommodation of small livestock such as fancy mice is a fairly simple matter; nothing elaborate is required. Any brick building, wooden shed, spare room or attic can be made suitable. The majority of fanciers have their mousery in the back garden in the form of a wooden shed, either self-built or purchased from one of the commercial companies, or in their cellar. Most fanciers have a shed in the region of 7' x 5' to 10' x 6', depending on individual circumstances. A shed of about this size will easily house several hundred mice if necessary and still leave ample space for supplies.

It is essential to the health of the occupants that the shed be kept dry and draft-proof. A good roof will last for years and it is easy to replace if leaks eventually begin. The transparent plastic type of roof is not recommended because it has poor insulation qualities, especially in very hot weather when the occupants may well be fried in the sun.

Probably the best type of wood is red cedar, although obviously this is not the cheapest. It will, however, last longest and will not suffer from shrinkage and cracks, which cause drafts. Many successful studs have been kept in tiny mouseries, but for the comfort of the fancier I would recommend as large a shed as possible. Also, a larger shed will not be subject to sudden temperature changes. If your shed is in the garden, it should be raised off the ground by at least 12 inches.

The author in his mousery. Note the stack of breeding boxes set on several tiers of racks and his work table at the left.

This prevents excess dampness in the shed and allows fresh air to circulate under the floorboards. Sheds can be expensive but will last a lifetime with these simple precautions.

Good ventilation for the occupants is most important. At least one window should be made to open. Mice are quite hardy, so the window can be left open at all times, except in extreme cold weather or when there is snow or fog. In the summer the door of the shed can also be opened during the day provided a wire-covered frame is put in its place to prevent the entry of stray cats, wild mice or rats. For the same reason, wire mesh, such as chicken or aviary wire, should be permanently fixed to the inside of the window(s) that open.

I believe that it is a good idea to insulate the walls and roof of the shed. This can be carried out in many ways. I personally have used fiber-glass insulation and have covered this with a decorative hard board for neatness. Some fanciers use heating of one form or another during the winter months, while others do not. The mice themselves, if healthy and well managed, should survive the severest winter without heating, although they may not breed quite as readily. I am not in favor of oil heaters because of the unhealthy smell and the danger of fire. Electric heating is probably best but is expensive. I really doubt that heating is necessary except for the comfort of the fancier.

Electric light is a necessity and this can easily be run from the house to the shed via a special weatherproof cable. A power receptacle would be advantageous as well, so that if an electric heater was required it could be safely used. In extreme hot weather an electric fan would certainly help to change the air. A cheaper method would be to sprinkle cold water on the floor; this helps a little to keep the air cooler.

The question of heating is a personal point and the

reader must decide for himself whether or not he wishes it. Bear in mind two points. Heating is an economically unsound proposition, for if it is to be effective it must be maintained throughout the cold months. Secondly, mice housed in such artificial luxuries will, when taken to shows, quickly lose their condition when subjected to a much lower temperature.

Planning the mousery is also something that reflects the tastes of the individual. There are no hard and fast rules to follow; I am merely trying to give guidelines. For example, a good solid table top is very useful, and it is best situated beneath a window so that the fancier can inspect his stock in natural light. A bag of sawdust, some hay and the food (the latter preferably in mouse-proof tins) should be kept under the table. Along the back of the shed can be stacked the mouse boxes, either on top of each other, on shelves or on racks. Linoleum on the floor completes the mousery, making it easier to sweep and keep clean and tidy.

A shed such as this will be a credit to the fancier and will make it easier for him to achieve good results.

5: Making Racks and Breeding Boxes

Before making breeding boxes, the fancier should consider how they will be stacked. Some do not use any kind of shelving at all, merely placing the boxes one on top of the other. This, of course, means that more boxes can be stacked in an area, but it is rather inconvenient if one requires the box at the bottom of the stack. Shelves are better but some food might be accidentally left on them, which can encourage vermin. The best method is some form of racking: 1½ inches x 1½ inches planed timber is an ideal size for racks. Two lengths of same size as the length of the shed will be required for each rack, plus two bearers approximately 18 inches in length. The two bearers should be securely screwed to the shed walls and then the two racks can be attached onto them. The bottom rack should be at least 6 inches off the shed floor in case any escapees have to be caught.

About 9 inches between each rack should be sufficient to take the weight of a mouse box. Assuming your shed is 8 feet in length, you ought to be able to get eight boxes on each rack. Obviously the weight of so many boxes will cause the racks to sag a bit, so cut 9-inch pieces of timber for use as vertical struts in the center of each rack. Racks built in such a manner will make it easy to reach any box required and have the further advantage of circulating fresh air around each box.

Materials like cotton, wool or other fibers are not safe as bedding. When these products are ingested intestinal blockage can occur and cause death. A Three Lions photo.

Many pet shops sell wood shavings for small mammals, such as mice, in packages of different weights and sizes. This product is convenient to use, clean and disposable. Photo by M. F. Roberts.

I think you will agree that you do not have to be a master craftsman to make racks as I have described them, and the same applies to making the actual cages for your mice. Any kind of box can be made suitable for mice because they are adaptable creatures and will survive quite well in almost anything, provided it is warm, dry and well ventilated. As far as the fancier is concerned, the important points to consider are accessability to the mice for inspection and feeding and ease of maintenance. Time has honored the use of the design of the mouse box described below. This type of box described lays no claim to being attractive but is popular because of its practicality.

Wood is undoubtedly the best material to use as it meets all the necessary requirements. Any kind of wood can be used—even plywood—provided it is at least a half inch thick. The size of the box can vary according to the timber available, but I would suggest 18 inches long x 9 inches wide x 6 inches high as being reasonable. Try to make the floor of one piece of wood; otherwise the sawdust will seep through any cracks, and it is possible that the mice wil also gnaw there as well; they seem to attack the cage floor more than any other part of the box. It will be worthwhile to paint the floor with a non-toxic paint, especially if it is plywood, to prevent undue soaking from urine. Painting can go about 1 inch up the sides, but there is no need to paint the entire box. Indeed, there is a case for leaving the wood bare so that it can "breathe" and retain its normal moisture content, so helping to prevent condensation. Floors can easily be replaced periodically when damage has been sustained.

Opposite:
Judge Jon Strutt of the British National Mouse Club casts his expert eyes over a Chinchilla.

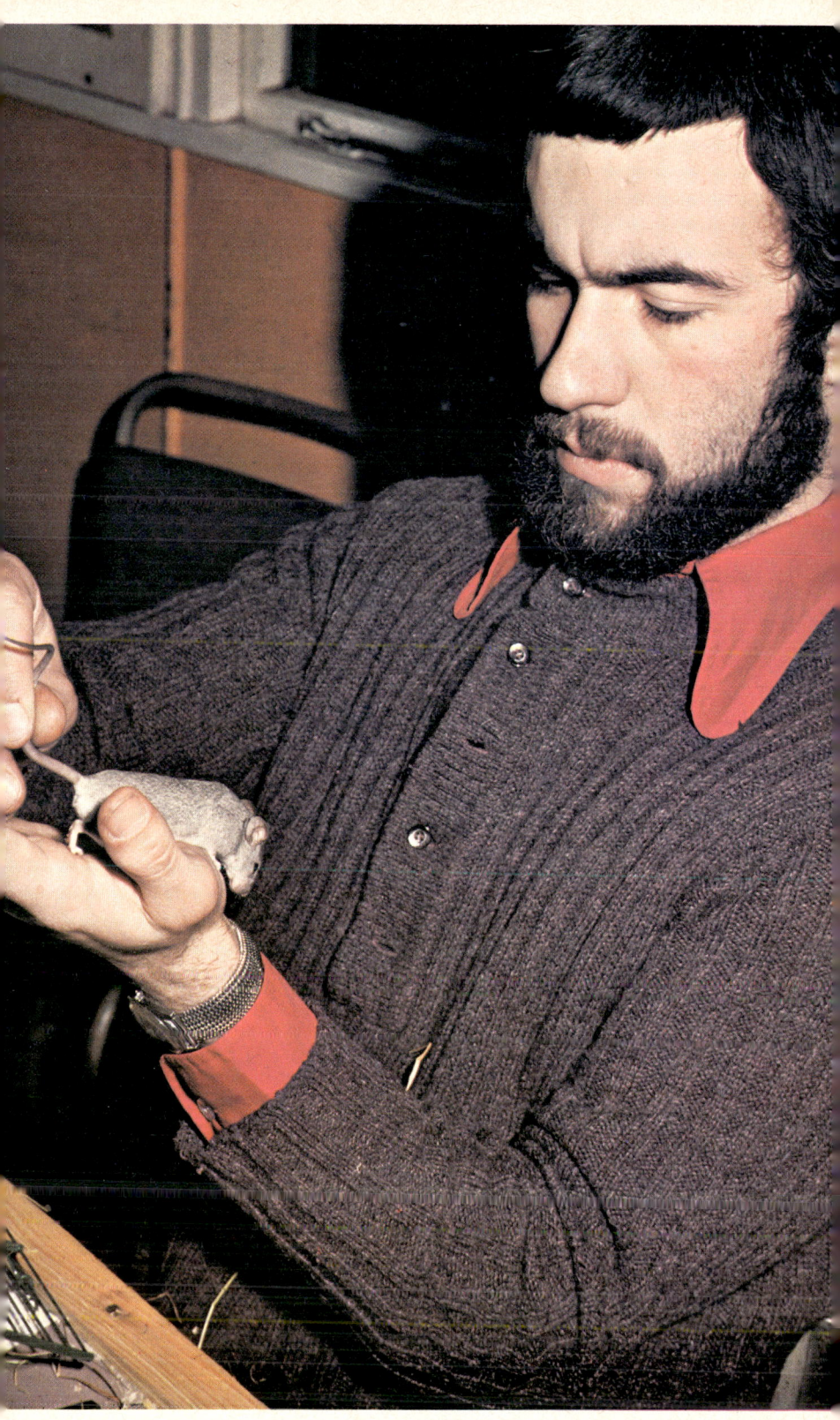

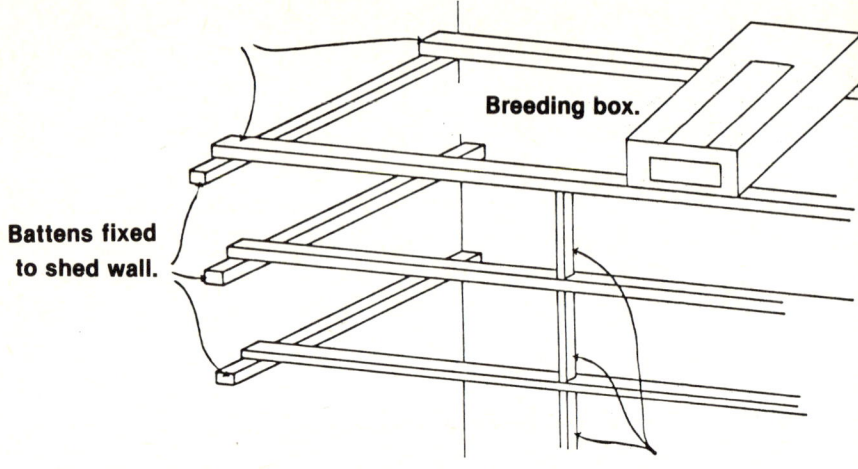

Diagram of timber racking attached to the wall of a shed or room.

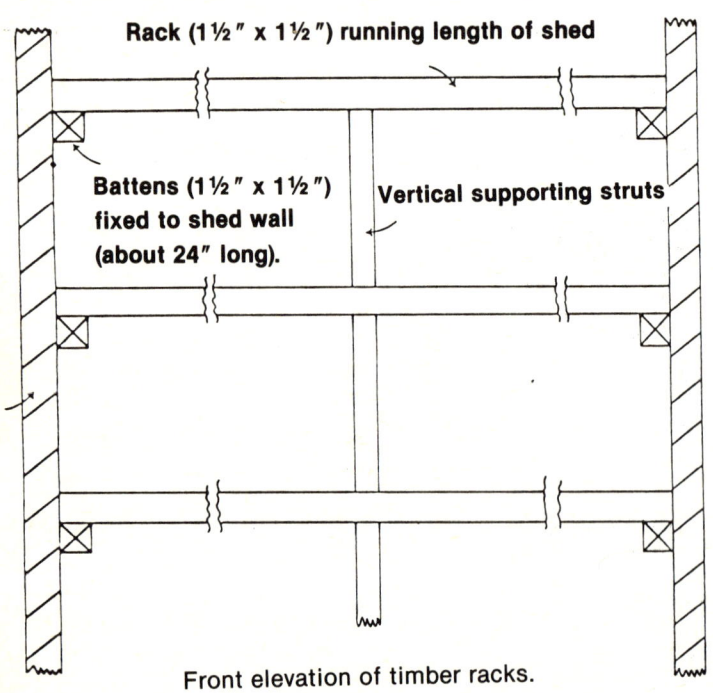

Front elevation of timber racks.

Thus for our mouse box we need two pieces of wood approximately 18 inches x 9 inches, one for the floor and one for the lid; two pieces 18 inches x 6 inches for the sides; and two pieces 9 inches x 6 inches for the front and back. A window should be cut into the front piece and covered with perforated zinc. Similarly a section of the lid should be cut out and covered. This enables fresh air to enter the box from the front and stale air to rise out at the top. Perforated zinc has one disadvantage in that the owner cannot see the occupants without opening the box. However, a wider gauge of ventilation, such as cage bird wires, has several disadvantages. For instance, young mice of, say 14 days, could easily escape through the wires. If wild mice did happen to enter the mousery, they could attack the pedigreed mice and possibly ruin a fine exhibition animal by tearing a piece out of an ear or biting off toes, toenails or the end of a tail. Surely nothing could be more disheartening. This could also occur if one of your own mice were on the loose overnight, especially if it were a buck. Unplanned matings through such open-wire bars have also been known to occur.

Finally, if I haven't convinced you already, insects, especially flies, cannot penetrate perforated zinc to lay eggs or spread diseases. Whatever kind of covering is used should be attached from the inside to prevent gnawing, as mice will always attack lighted areas. The four sides should be nailed to the floor and a further piece of wood the width of the box and about 3 inches high should be fixed to the rear one quarter to form the nesting compartment. On the other hand, a complete and removable nest box can be made and is certainly easier to clean. Also, the mice will tend to chew it rather than the box itself. Finally, two battens should be nailed to the underside of the lid to prevent lateral movement. We now have a completed breeding box.

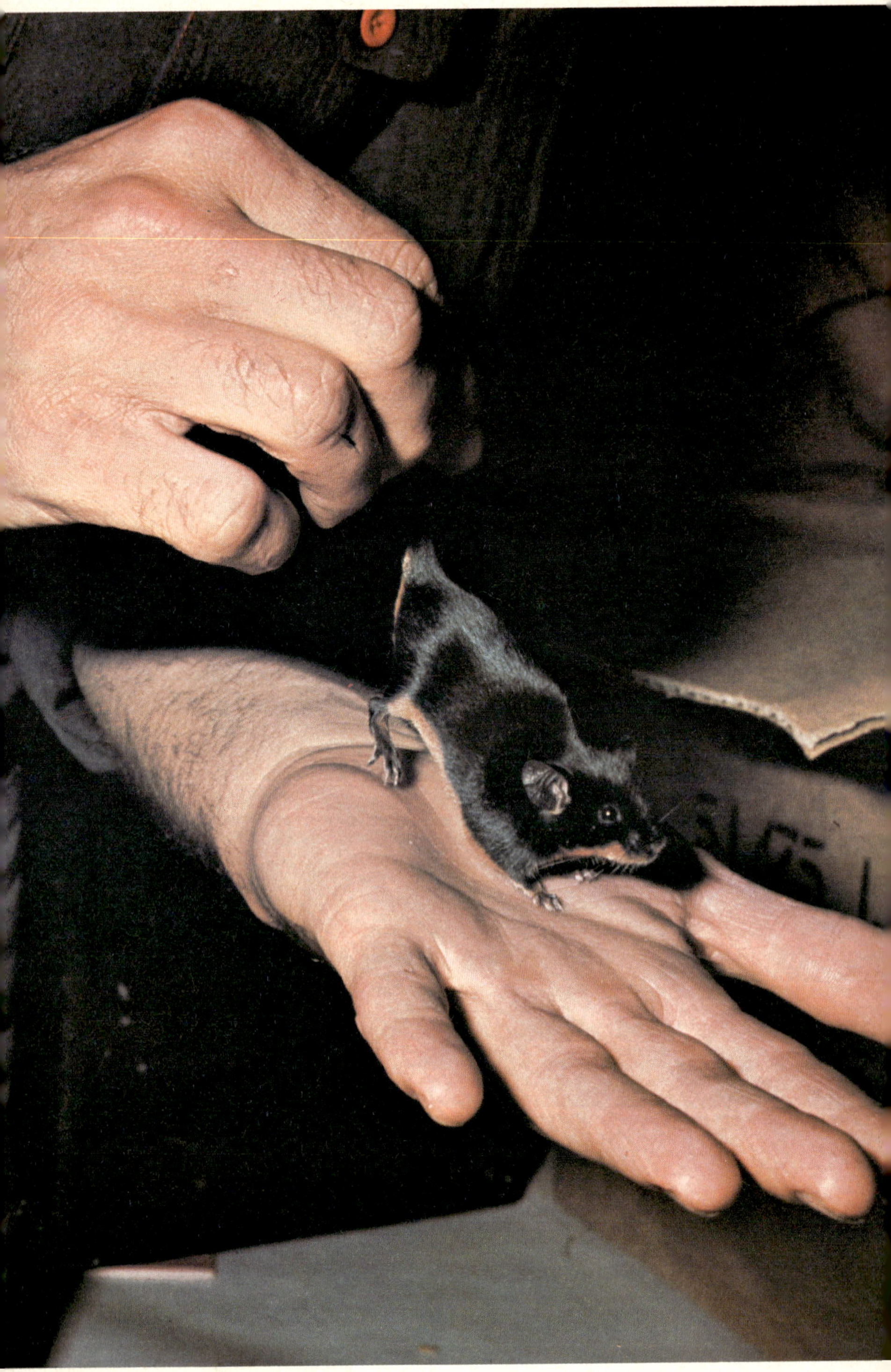

This is not the recommended way of holding a mouse.

Opposite:
This is the correct way to hold a mouse.

One cannot be dogmatic in dealing with the question of breeding boxes for exhibition mice. As long as the five following points are adhered to, any design will suit:
1) Reasonable size
2) Good ventilation
3) Strong material to prevent gnawing
4) Not too heavy to be handled
5) Easy to clean out

Most fanciers have one or two boxes a good deal larger than the standard size for running of young stock, does that are between matings or exhibition stock. The normal size of box is ideal for a breeding trio or for one or two does to raise a litter. The maximum number of adults I would suggest for such a box would be six. Any more than this number would result in overcrowded conditions. It is remarkable that mice, having been used to roaming in the wild state, can remain so fit in such comparatively small homes, yet they certainly do. I am all in favor of large boxes, especially for young and growing stock. More living space helps them to keep more fit and enhances their maximum growth potential (provided they are fed correctly). I have one reservation with the extremely large boxes: the mice become used to running and leaping about so much that they become rather difficult to manage. Being hard to handle will certainly be a handicap to general management and especially on the show bench where the mouse will not show itself to advantage if it is "jumpy." I would suggest a size approximately 30 inches x 12 inches x 10 inches high as being suitable for placing a number of youngsters or adult does together. Do not overcrowd the youngsters (and keep the young bucks separate from the does) or you will defeat the purpose of letting them build up their muscle and growth potential. Ten pups

A rack that is slightly modified in construction; wider planks of wood are used for shelvings instead of simple battens. Photo by A.P. May.

would be about right, although you could put a few more together.

You can experiment with the construction of these types of cages. If glass fronts are constructed, you can view your stock with ease, but remember to provide a good deal of ventilation. Always try to have a few spare cages available in case of emergencies. Once a year a batch at a time can be scrubbed, disinfected and left to dry in the sun before being used again.

39

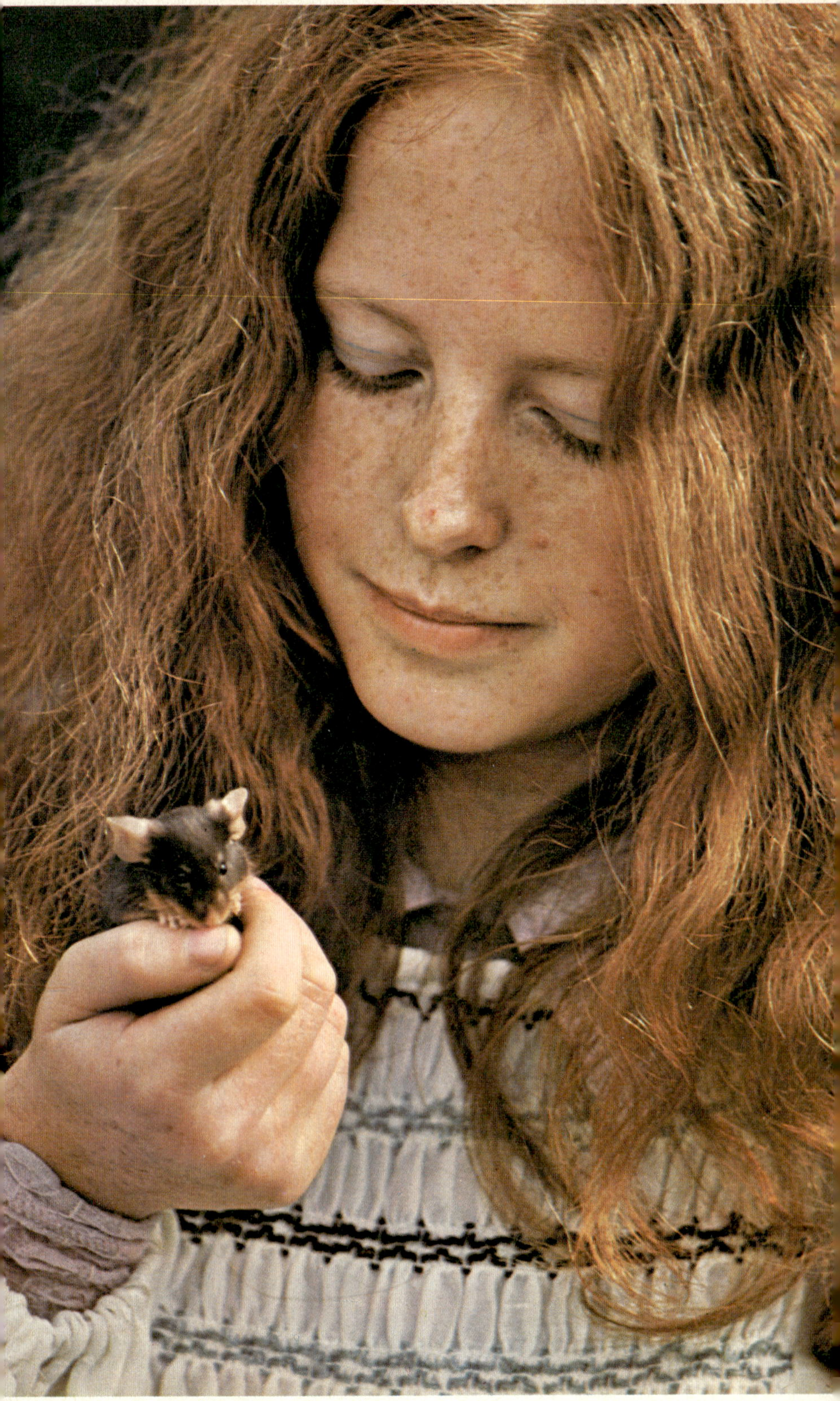

A Self Cream with black eyes. Note the large eyes, a feature considered important in this variety. **Below:** A Himalayan with red eyes. The body is white and the points are light brown. **Opposite:** With proper care and management, keeping mice in the home should not be objectionable for anyone, young or old.

6: Bedding

The floor of the mouse box should have a good covering of clean, dry sawdust. This will soak up the urine. Place a large handful of hay or paper shavings in the nesting compartment. The hay must be of good quality—sweet smelling and not stalky. It would be fatal to use damp, musty or mildewy hay. Even the best hay has some dust in it; this should be shaken out before being placed in the boxes. Paper shavings are certainly cleaner but have no food value; mice love to chew on hay but will not chew paper shavings. If you are keeping whites for exhibition, you must use paper shavings that won't cause staining. Not only is hay a good natural food, it is also a wonderful conditioner. The mice will tunnel through it, and their coats will gleam beautifully. It is important at all times to replenish the nesting material wherever necessary. The mice use the nest as protection against the cold much the same way as we use blankets when we sleep. The nest will usually be open in warm weather, but when winter comes a tight nest will be constructed. Warmth from the bodies is kept within the nest, as you will discover for yourself if you chase out the occupants and place a finger inside. A piece of newspaper will help to keep the mice warm during severe weather, since they wil quickly shred it to line the nest. This should not be used for those mice you may be intending to exhibit, as the print may soil the coats, especially the lighter varieties. In damp weather

Hay is used in the Maxey cages. Hay keeps the mouse comfortable by serving as a padding against the cold metal surface and allows the mouse to tunnel in for a feeling of security.

the sawdust and hay will retain a high content of moisture that is in the air. It will pay dividends if the bedding is dried out in front of a fire before it is placed with the livestock. After all, how would you like to put on damp socks?

Except for does with newly-born litters, the boxes should be cleaned out once a week and fresh bedding supplied. Use a small paint scraper for cleaning out the bedding to ensure that no mess is left in the corners which the mice use for a toilet. In fact, these corners can be cleaned out more often than once a week. The rubbish is emptied into a bin which is then taken as refuse. Alternatively it can be burnt or used for compost in the garden.

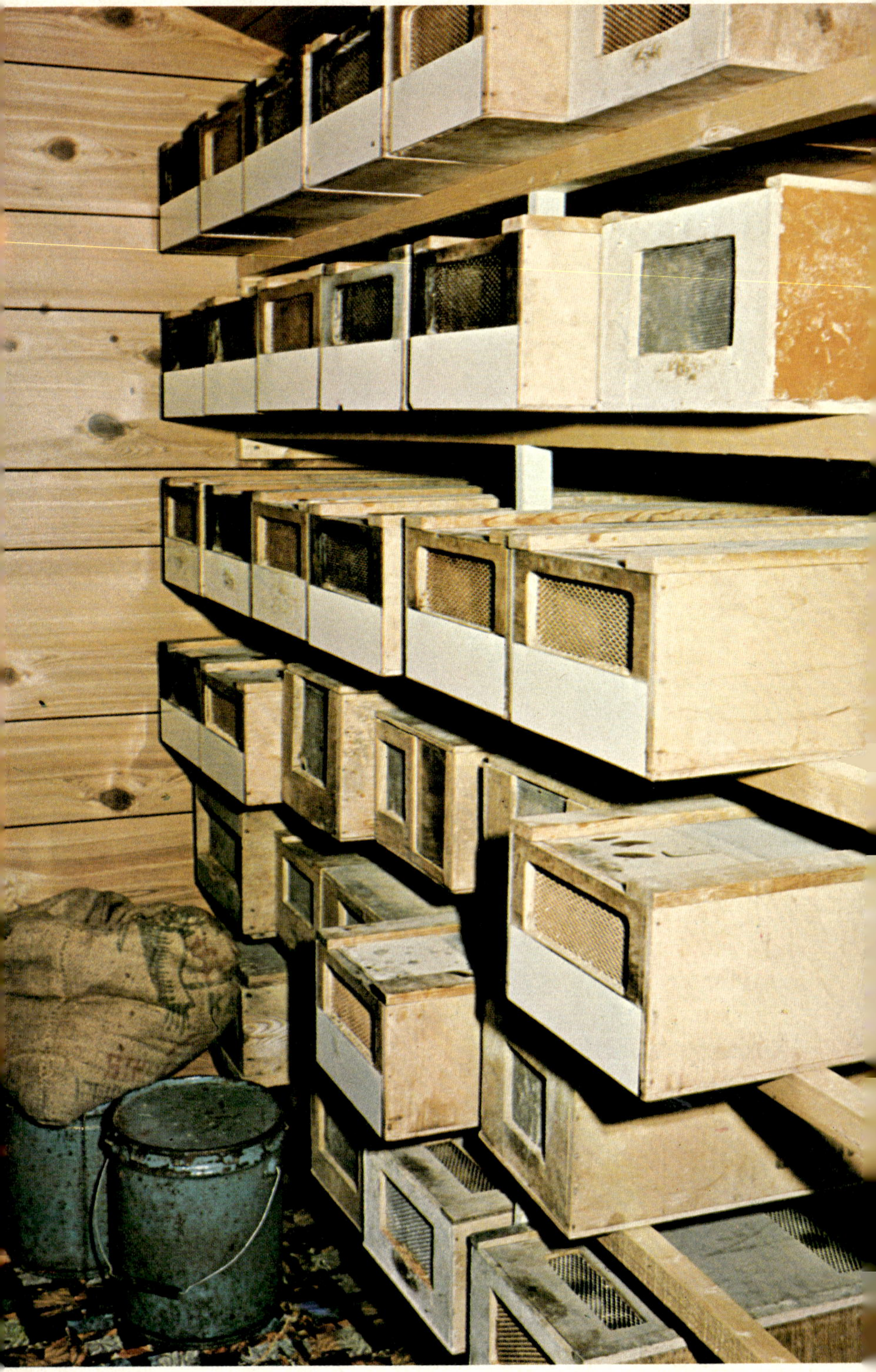

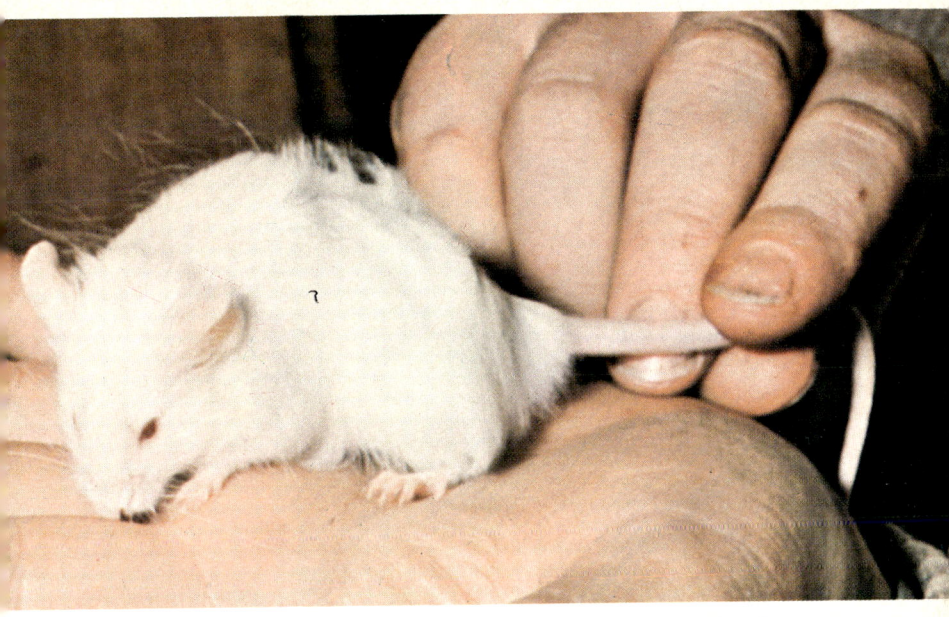

A Long-Haired White mouse. Other color varieties, like Creams, Silvers, Champagnes and Argentes, can carry the long hair factor also. **Below:** A Pink-Eyed Self Silver mouse. The standard allows black eyes in Silver, but such a specimen is still not known. **Opposite:** A view of the author's mousery showing the racks, breeding boxes and containers for holding seeds.

7: Feeding

In animal husbandry, feeding is of the utmost importance, for it not only serves to keep the captive animal alive but also affects general health, breeding and exhibition results.

Every mouse fancier has his own method of feeding, although most follow a basically similar pattern. The important thing is to feed regularly—once a day and at a certain time. The majority feed around eight o'clock in the evening; this is an ideal time for mice, who are just awakening for their nocturnal jaunts. However, mice will soon adapt to whatever feeding time is convenient for the fancier.

When the novice first purchases stock he should ask how they were fed and then follow that method for a while. This should prevent any upset stomachs, for mice easily lose condition through incorrect feeding. It has been my experience that most novices do not feed incorrectly, but more often than not they feed insufficiently. It is difficult, if not impossible, to overfeed mice (excepting those that are genetically more robust, e.g., Self Reds and Sables), because they do not gorge. I would prefer to waste food rather than have hungry livestock, so put in more food than you think is necessary and take out any perishable fodder the following evening. Eventually, experience will be your best judge in determining the amount of food to be fed.

Mice in the wild state will eat almost anything they come across, although they prefer grain and root crops.

Different types of seeds provide specific nutrients, and only the fancier knows what his show mice need. Products sold in pet shops as food for mice have been specifically formulated with the nutritional needs of the animals in mind. Photo by H.V. Lacey.

47

A Broken mouse; the example shown is not a good specimen.

A Rex mouse. The Rex is a comparatively new variety.

These baby Creams have been bred by the author and are about 9 to 10 days old. Notice that at this stage the eyes are still unopened.

An unidentified variety of mouse from a local pet shop. Photo by Dr. H.R. Axelrod.

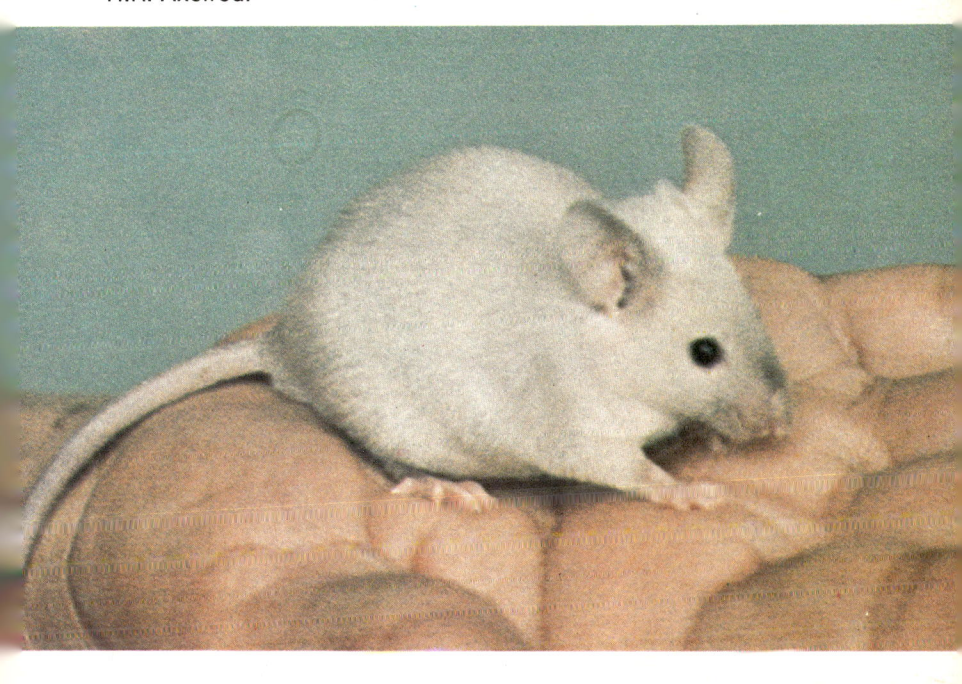

We, as their keepers, must ensure that a sensible and complete diet is given to our captive animals. Over the years fanciers have found that the best all-around basic diet for mice is clipped oats and stale bread with added moisture. A large handful of oats should be placed on the sawdust in each box. The bread should be about two or three days old so that it is slightly stale but not moldy. It can be broken up, placed in a bowl and soaked for about ten minutes in cold water. Then it should be squeezed out and left for another ten minutes to swell. Milk should be added and the bread can then be placed on top of the oats. Brown bread is preferable to white, although if the former is unobtainable, add bran to the mash. Some fanciers use glazed pots for the bread on the grounds of hygiene, but I have found this to be a waste of time. The mice seem to have no respect for their food in pots and take great delight in filling the pots with sawdust and using it as a toilet!

There is a difference of opinion as to whether or not to give water. Although I do not give water myself (the mice obtain ample moisture from bread and milk), I believe it can do only good. Pots are out, of course, but water bottles obtained from the local pet shops are ideal.

Aside from the above basic diet there are various other types of food that can be given. If clipped oats are in short supply, crushed oats can be substituted, although they are not as useful for keeping the adult animal's teeth occupied. Crushed oats are beneficial to babies just leaving the nest. To vary the diet, the fancier can give a little wheat, sunflower seed or white millet. The last two seeds are good conditioners, and sunflower seeds especially are a strong favorite with most mice. Wheat is very useful, especially in winter, but it should be given sparingly as it can cause overheating of the bloodstream. This is evident in the ears of the mouse,

A gravity-feed waterer is an ingenious method of providing clean water at all times. Water is licked at the outflow tube whenever desired by the mouse or rat.

which turn slightly red, but the condition is not serious and will disappear in 24 hours. Maize and hemp are also rich and can cause skin troubles, so they should only be given in extremely cold weather. Wheat can be given all year round.

Dog biscuits can be left in the cage at all times to give the mice something to chew on and so keep their teeth in use. Similarly, some bread can be baked until it is as hard as a rock to serve the same purpose. Any dry biscuit from the larder, or any cereal that has no sugar, such as cornflakes, will be readily eaten. Once a week a raw egg can be added to the bread and milk mash. I add a few drops of cod liver oil, which helps keep out the cold in winter.

A typical breeding box with the lid removed. Wood chips and hay are used for lining the bottom of the box.

All the necessary equipment for breeding, keeping and showing mice can all be kept in the shed. The large black cases behind the author are travelling boxes for transporting mice.

For pregnant does, a little vitamin/mineral supplement can be sprinkled on the mash every other day during pregnancy. When the litter has its eyes open, sprinkle a little on the nest for them to start eating. To facilitate bone growth, add some calcium phosphate to the mash of pregnant does and to that of all growing youngsters until they are 12 weeks of age.

Some fanciers give green food to their mice, others never do. If you decide to give greens, be careful at first if your stock has never had greens before; otherwise diarrhea will result. Also ensure that the greens given are perfectly clean and not contaminated. Greens that can safely be given include dandelion, chickweed, young grass shoots and cauliflower leaves. I have known fanciers to give table scraps, meat, chicken bones and bacon rind. Others feed poultry laying mash with good results. Thus, the diet for mice can be extremely varied and will largely depend on what the mice are used to and what the fancier finds convenient to feed.

The beginning and intermediate mouse fancier who does not have access to the feeds already mentioned would find it both convenient to himself and pleasing to his mice if he purchased a feed formula at his local pet shop. Such brand-name mixtures generally contain the basic nutritional ingredients necessary for the proper growth and development of mice. Many fanciers have successfully raised their mice on commercial, not homemade, foods.

8: Breeding

Mice reach maturity at approximately 12 weeks of age; at this time they can be placed in the breeding boxes. Although they will certainly mate as early as five or six weeks, it is, of course, bad practice to allow this. Mice should be mated by the age of 16 weeks, otherwise some difficulty may result in producing decent litters. Bucks may be used at ten weeks, if necessary, although they should not be taxed. If you have a good stud buck who continually turns out decent youngsters, he can be used until he grows visibly old and loses his virility. Does, however, do not last very long because (quite apart from genetic influences) the growth of the suckling litter is powerfully influenced by environmental factors, in particular the amount of milk available. An old doe cannot produce the same milk yield as a doe in her prime, so the lesson is obvious: never breed a mouse over one year old. I would say that three litters is the maximum to expect from one doe.

Most animals are at their best with their second litters, do not despair if the first mating is unsuccessful; try again, preferably with a different sire. Mice mate very quickly and are very rarely sterile. Ovulation takes place over a period of four to six days, and the period of heat lasts about 12 hours. Once the does are placed with the buck, you can guess fairly accurately when the litters are due, for mating will occur almost immediately.

A food mixture for mice which includes oats, sunflower seeds and dog biscuit.

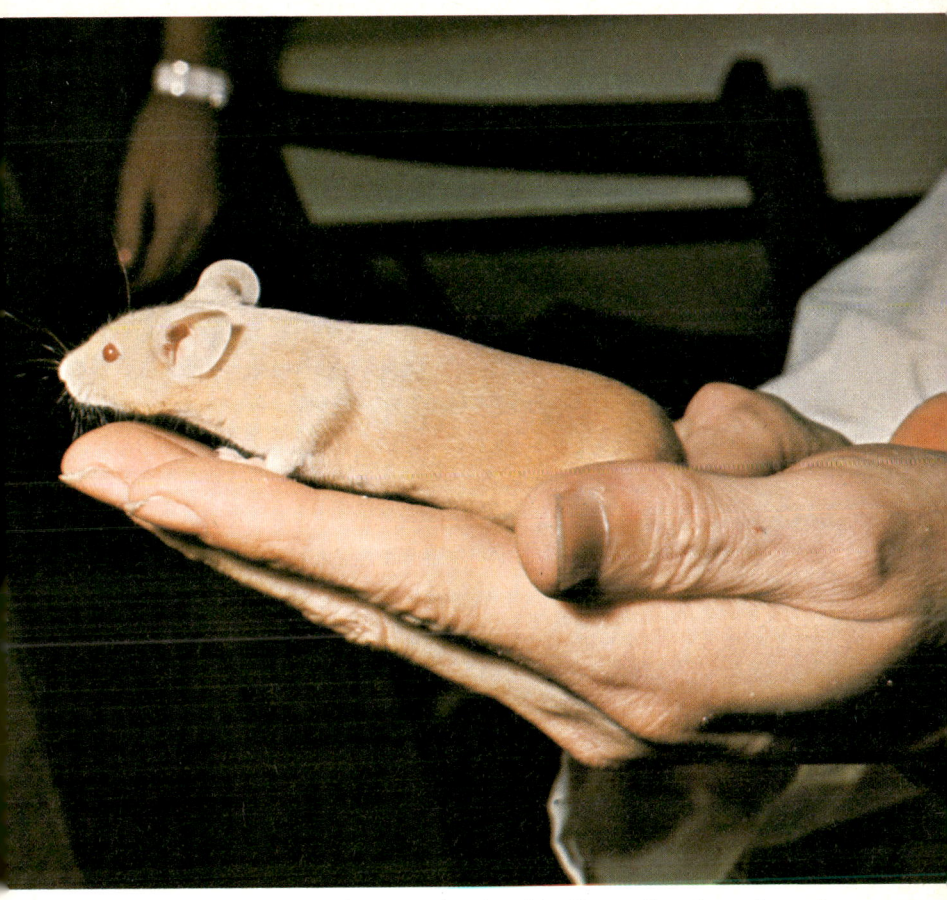

This fancy mouse, an Argente doe bred by the author, is a champion and winner of the Mendel Gold Cup.

The gestation period is between 18 and 21 days. At approximately 14 days it will be quite obvious when a doe is in kindle, and the buck should then be removed. It is quite permissible to let two or three does kindle together for they will happily suckle each other's young in a communal nest. However, it is important that they kindle within a day or two of each other; otherwise the last born will have to struggle against its older and stronger companions to obtain a full milk supply. Does may also be removed and placed in separate boxes, if there are enough to spare. In this way the breeder can ensure a good mother-litter relationship. Personally, I prefer two does littering together in case one is a bad mother, and also because the litter receives twice the attention and is always kept warm by one or the other. The buck should not be left alone for more than two nights or he will lose condition, nor can he be placed with other bucks, so he should be placed in a fresh box with new does. He can be exposed to a maximum of four does at any one time; otherwise the buck will become taxed. Never put bucks into a cage already occupied, or they may be resented and attacked by the does. Most animals have a sense of "territory" and attack invaders of whatever sex. Therefore, use unoccupied cages when placing strangers together and all will be well.

Do not handle pregnant does, if possible, during the last week of pregnancy. Make sure they receive extra bedding and plenty of food, especially wheat germ and calcium phosphate with bread and milk mash. The aim is to produce large babies at birth so that they will develop into large adults.

When the litter has been born, carefully inspect and dispose of any dead babies. There may be as few as two or three babies or as many a 18 but the average is approximately eight to ten, which is ideal. Too few babies could indicate lack of fertility; too many means

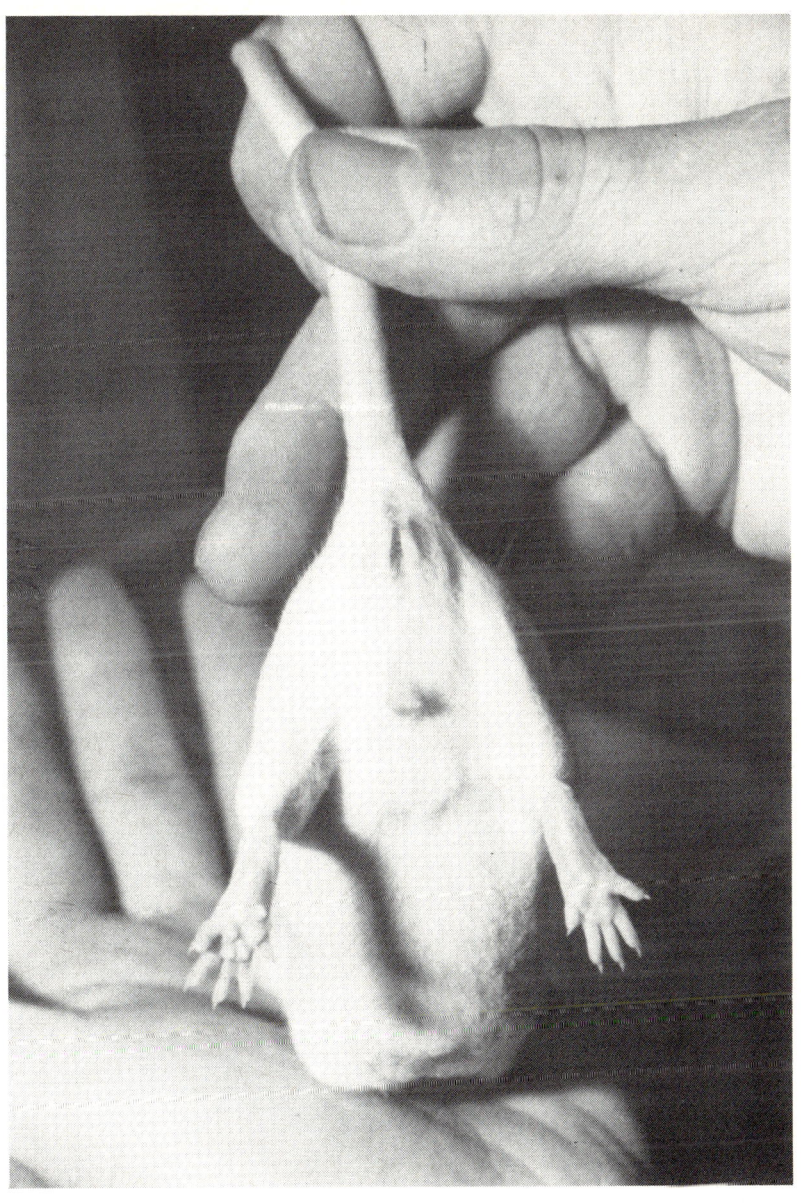

Ventral view of a male mouse. Identifying the sexes in mice is not too difficult even at an early age.

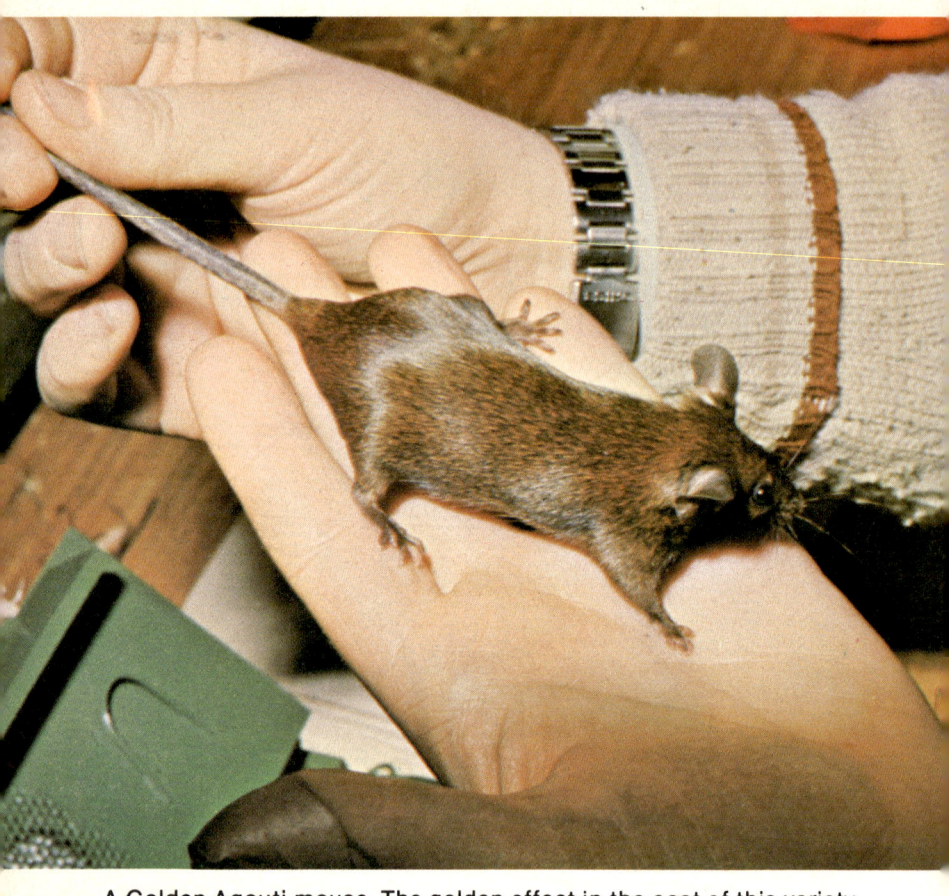

A Golden Agouti mouse. The golden effect in the coat of this variety is achieved by having yellow pigment in only some of the hairs.

Opposite:
A breeding box with several Satins. Satin are easy to identify; the metallic sheen of the coat is very characteristic.

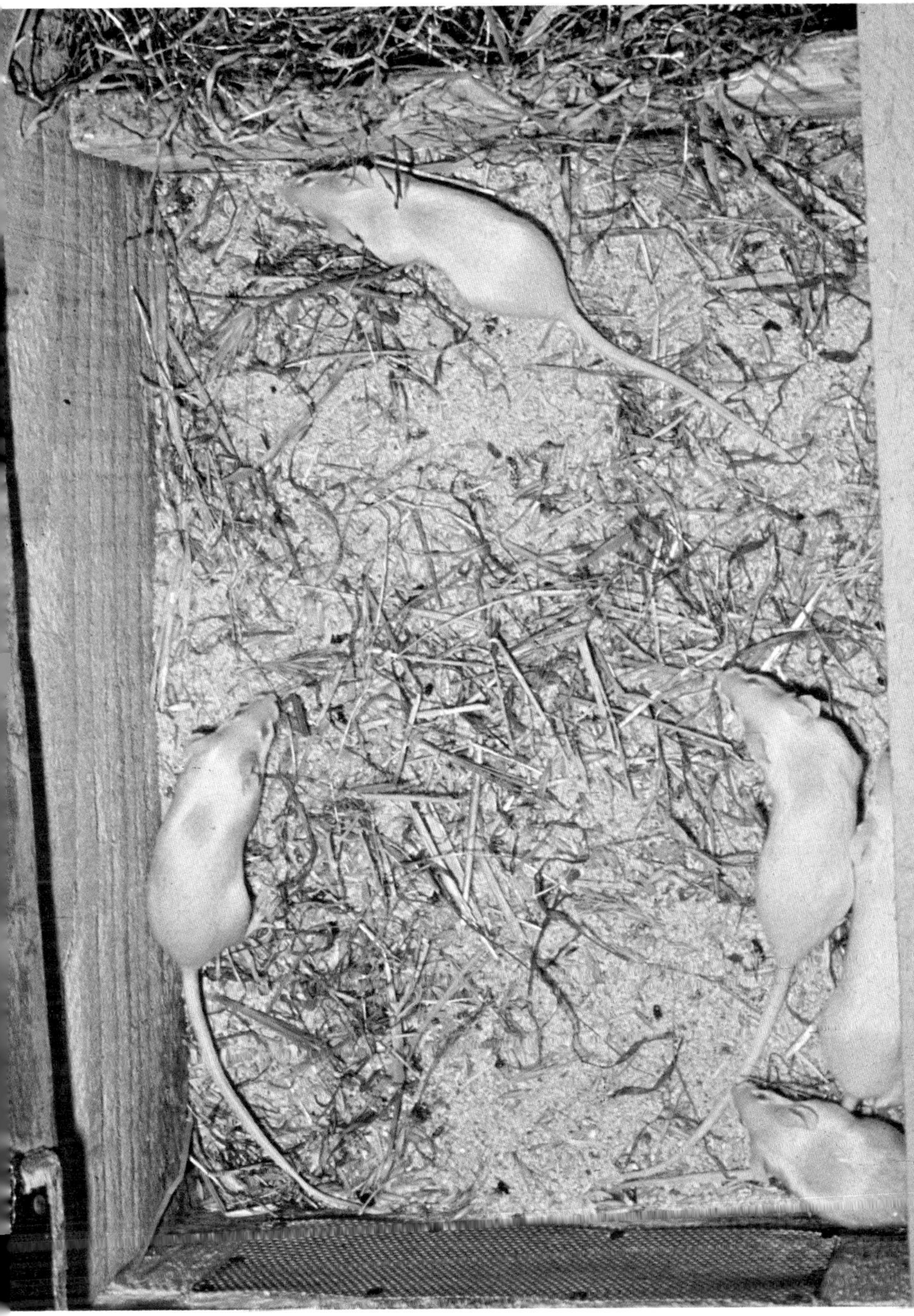

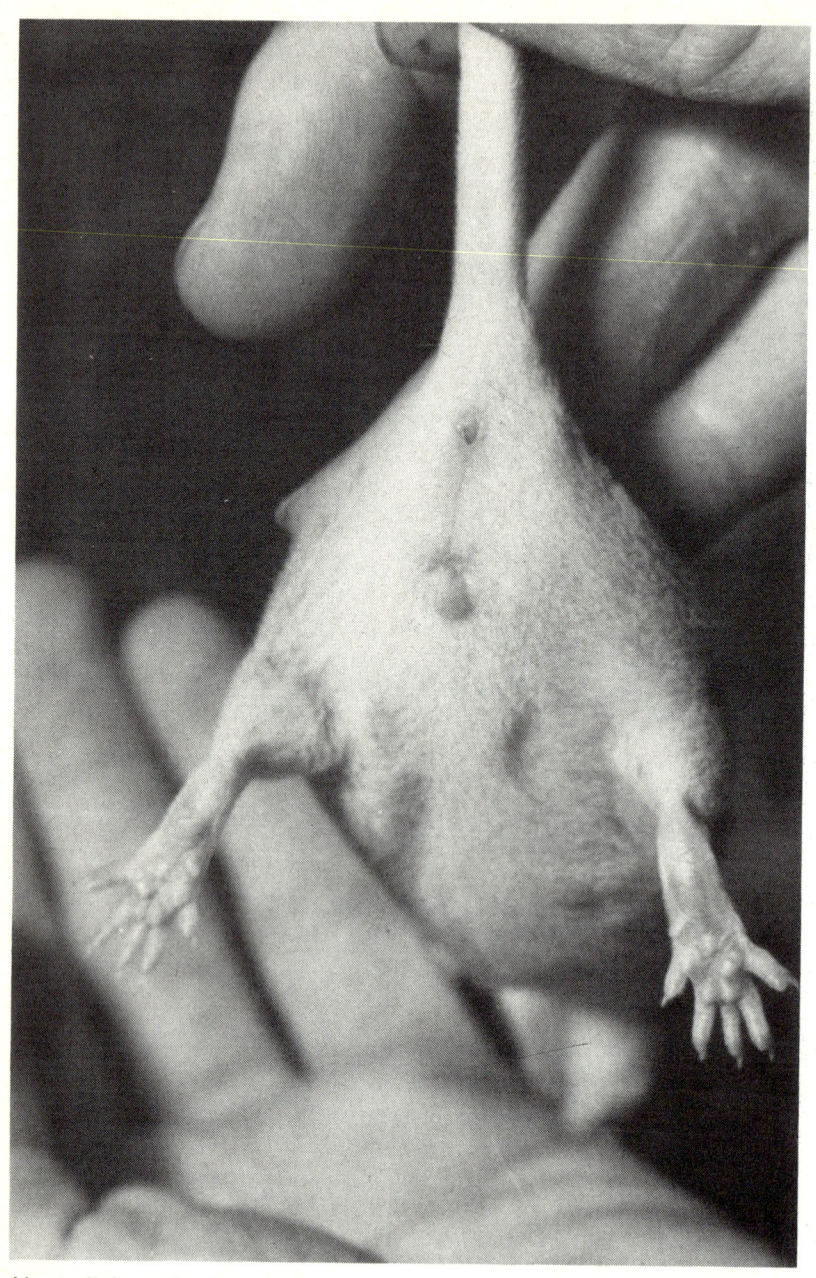

Ventral view of a female mouse. Females also have a row of nipples on each side of the abdomen.

that they will be correspondingly small and may not develop into big adults. The doe can be taken out while the nest is inspected, although this is not absolutely necessary since most does do not seem to mind interference provided they are used to being handled often. It would be wise to rub your fingers in a soiled corner so that you have the mother's scent, and no other, when touching the babies.

Newly born mice are completely helpless creatures, naked and blind. They rely entirely on the mother's milk to survive. It is unfortunately a cruel necessity that if we are to ensure that our fancy mouse reaches its full potential of size and health, a reduction in the size of the litters has to be carried out. This task is known as "culling" and is a matter of destroying the smallest individuals of every litter until only the best three or four remain.

The litter should be left alone for three days because the doe's milk production increases with the number of sucking young. The runts of the litter should be the first to go, then any with thin or kinked tails or narrow skulls. The quickest and most humane method to destroy babies is to throw them hard upon a stone floor. This is not a pleasant task, but be assured they will die instantly. The hair begins to grow after a few days so that color and markings can be seen, and then further culling should take place with any that are mismarked or of poor color. This should be done gradually; about ten days later there should be only three or four mice left.

It is mainly because this culling process has been the rule over the years that fancy mice are so exceptional for size and fitness. Therefore, culling should be thought of not as destroying life but as helping those left to survive better. Culling can be useful for keeping down the number of bucks, for the breeder will not require many

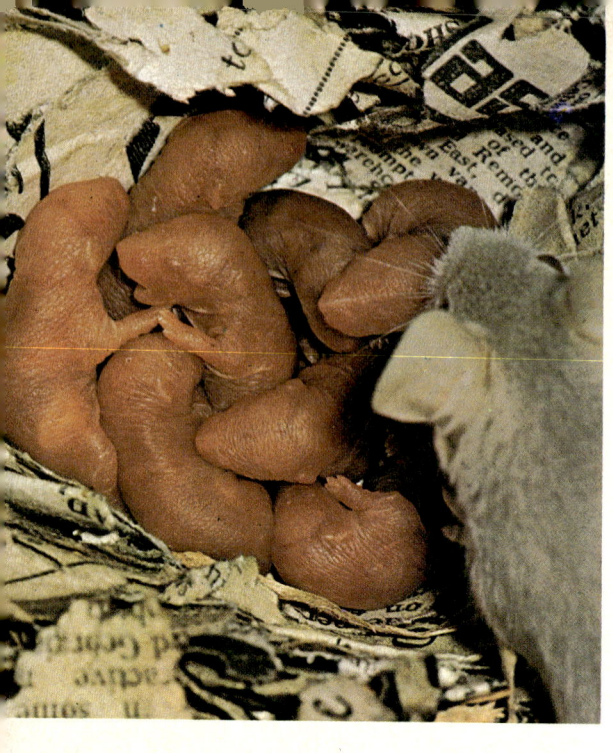

Newly born mice are very helpless; they are naked and their eyes are closed.

A mother mouse watching her litter of young Whites that are about 7 days old.

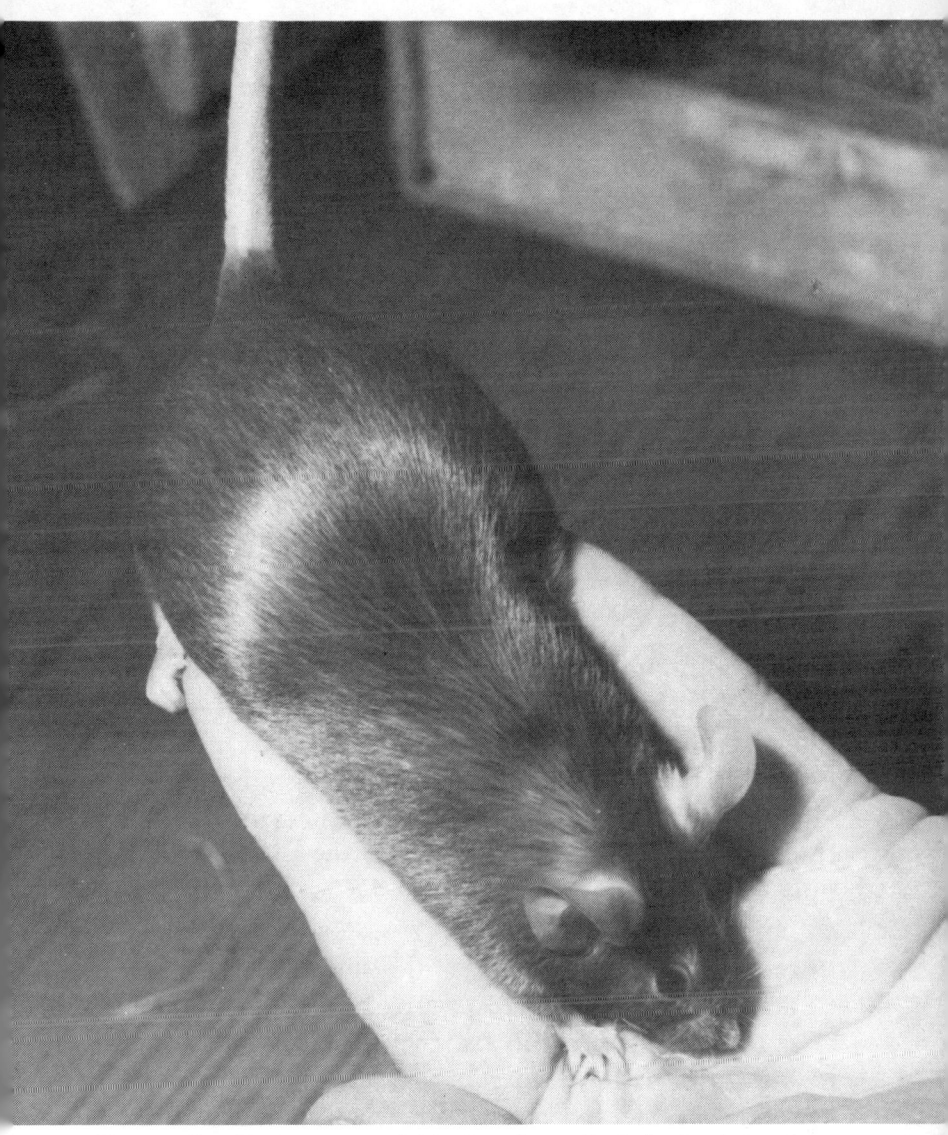

The swollen hindquarters of this doe shows that she is obviously expecting a litter soon.

a. Buck   b. Doe

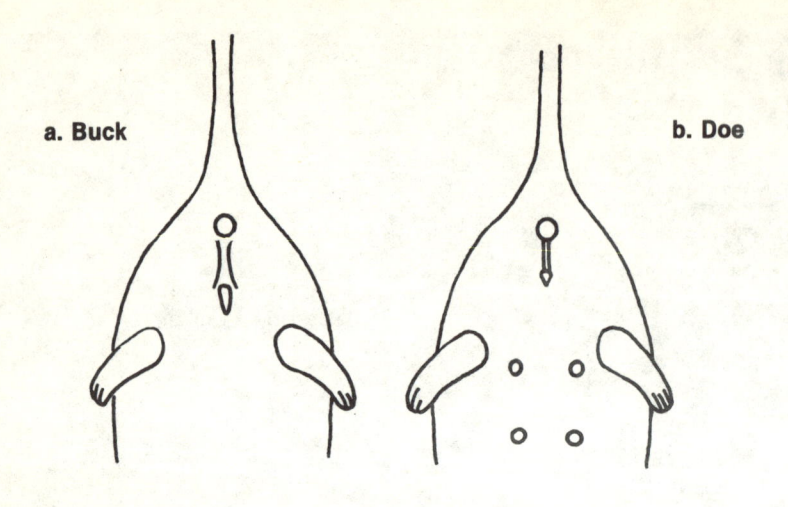

Diagrammatic illustration of the abdomen of a buck (a) and doe (b).

in his stud. With experience, it is a simple matter to sex babies, although it is difficult to describe the difference in words. If possible, visit an experienced fancier's mousery and ask him for a demonstration. Once knowledgeable on this point, the novice can then raise either all bucks or all does in a litter. The reason for this is that the birth weight in males is greater than in females and unless given a fair chance the latter have difficulty catching up to the stronger, greedier males. Thus we have two valid reasons for culling bucks.

Mice are precocious creatures and can reach puberty at five weeks. For this reason the young bucks should be separated from their mothers and/or sisters. At this age they can be placed with other young bucks until the best are required for stud purposes. Young mice should be handled frequently from an early age until they are six to seven weeks old and ready for exhibiting in the young classes; at this time they are perfectly manageable and show their good points off to advantage.

9: Fostering

At one time or another it may be necessary for the breeder to foster the whole or part of a litter from one doe to another. Fostering can be useful during breeding operations if, for example, you have an exceptional doe from whom you require the maximum of litters. Thus some, or even all, of her youngsters can be fostered to proven brood does. In this way there is no danger of culling what might have turned out to be a champion, but it goes without saying that many runts should still be culled.

If the doe is relieved of all her babies and given a week's rest, she can be returned to a different buck and the process continued. Good foster does are obviously those mice of the larger varieties such as P.E. Whites, Silvers and B.E. Creams. If you are fostering black eyed babies use P.E. fostering mothers; in this way you will not be confused, for the babies of the foster mother will be of different eye color.

The foster does should be mated at the same time as the doe from whom we require the desired litter. Once all the does have given birth, the mothers should be removed while the change-over takes place. Gently rub each baby with a little of the foster mother's soiled litter so that she cannot detect a strange scent. The foster mother can then be replaced in the bedding box and given something to eat. In most cases there should be no trouble whatsoever.

These baby mice are twelve days old. The eyes should be open soon, and in 20 days they can be weaned and sexed. Photo by Harry V. Lacey.

Another method of fostering is to mate your good doe and then introduce two foster does a day or so later. The foster does will give birth after the good doe, in which case their babies will be easy to sort out and destroy as they will be smaller. The good doe can then be taken away and the fosters will successfully raise her litter. Fostering is especially useful with those varieties that are smaller than average. This applies particularly to the marked varieties, such as the Dutch.

10: Ailments

Fortunately this chapter will be a short one, for fancy mice are reasonably free from diseases. This is due to the high standard of health that breeders have placed upon their breeding stock in the past. Even the very best exhibition mice are not worth keeping if they are overtaken by illness. Because mice are so short-lived, it is best to destroy any stricken victims. In fact it is extremely difficult and can be expensive to care for an ill mouse. Mice are not worth a lot of money individually, and the breeder can reproduce any good specimen, so it is best to destroy stock which is unhealthy. Drowning and gassing are not the most humane methods of destroying mice. The quickest and most efficient method, as mentioned earlier, is to hold the mouse by the tail and throw it very hard, head first, upon a hard substance. Death will be instantaneous.

DIARRHEA

This ailment is usually apparent in young stock but is rarely serious. It can be caused by bad management, sour milk or wet greenfood. Arrowroot in powder or biscuit form should quickly clear up the trouble. If not, the young mice affected will have to be destroyed, because they will not develop into strong adults.

TUMORS

These cancerous growths occur mostly on elderly mice. There is no cure, and in fact the mice affected may be suffering, so it is for the best that they be put out of their misery. Some kinds of tumors are hereditary, so do not breed mice with growths.

PARASITES

All livestock is subject to parasites of one form or another. Fancy mice rarely suffer from such pests, although parasites may breed in cracks in the boxes or in the dust of the hay or seeds. Tiny blood-sucking parasites are most commonly found on babies in the nest and can be destroyed with a safe insect powder available from the local pet shop.

ASTHMA

This is the most frequent complaint in fancy mice. No one has a cure and no one really is certain what it is or what causes it. "Asthma" is a misnomer, although the mice apparently suffer from some form of bronchial malady. It can occur in any mousery at any time, although it is prevalent in damp winter conditions. The novice can detect it by listening for a strange clicking or whistling sound emitted by the victims. The affected mice should be destroyed immediately or the ailment may spread like a common cold throughout the shed. Some fanciers admit to curing affected mice by smearing camphorated oil on the sides and lids of the boxes, but I have my doubts about this cure.

A possible *cause* of asthma in mice is damp, dirty or diseased hay, so obviously such an environment should be guarded against. It would be a blessing if we knew more of this disease, but the cost of discovering more about it via the laboratory would be prohibitive. I have discovered that a similar "wheezing" defect can occur in any livestock such as cattle, rabbits and dogs, but I'm afraid I have no conclusive answer.

The mouse shown above (perched on its owner's head) has clear, bright eyes; in the photo below, the fur is shiny and smooth, and an alert disposition is very evident.

11: "A Day at a Show is a Tonic"

After having bred your first litters you will want to exhibit at the earliest opportunity to discover how good your stock is. However you may fare, you will never forget your first exhibiting experience.

The only equipment the beginner needs to commence exhibiting with are Maxey show cages and a travelling box. You will need one Maxey for each exhibit, and I would suggest four to six would be more than sufficient together with a travelling box to accommodate this number. Maxey cages should all be of one design, size and color and should not have any identifiable marks which could be seen by the judge; otherwise your entry could be disqualified. The owner's name and address should be written underneath the Maxey for identification.

At shows held under N.M.C. patronage, all mice *must* be exhibited in Maxey pattern cages painted middle Brunswick green outside and royal or signal red inside. The only allowance made in the design of these show cages is that lids are optional. Maxey cages can be made by the fancier, although they are so cheap that it may be just as well to purchase them ready-made. There are no rules for the design of travelling boxes, although they should be sturdy and well ventilated.

Mouse shows are not actually run by the N.M.C., but by local clubs who rent a location, advertise the

Close-up of a Maxey cage with the lid raised in order to show the inner construction.

show and put up the prize money. The N.M.C. is merely the governing body which ensures that all mouse shows are run properly. If N.M.C. judges are engaged and guaranteed prize money is ensured, any individual or society can organize a mouse show with N.M.C. support.

There are various forms of shows, namely table shows, open shows and champion shows. The table shows are small affairs where prize money is paid out on a "sweepstake" basis, for example 75% of the entry fees. These shows are usually run by small local clubs and are ideal for beginners to learn about the facets of exhibiting, stewarding and judging. Open shows are, as

73

A travelling box is indispensable for transporting mice safely and conveniently. The one shown here can hold as many as eight Maxey cages at a time.

An impressive array of cups and ribbons awarded to different categories of winners.

the name implies, shows in which anyone can enter, irrespective of whether or not they are a member of the club organizing the event or of the N.M.C. Championship shows are those occasional events that warrant the "Blue Ribbon" status where entries are usually over the 1,000 mark.

At the majority of shows there are usually three or four N.M.C. judges handing out the awards, but at championship events there may be as many as seven top judges. At all shows, prize cards are awarded from first (red cards) to fourth (green cards) to C (Commended), HC (Highly Commended) and VCH (Very Highly Commended). These last three are white cards and are known to fanciers as "codding cards." At all shows accepted by the N.M.C., Specials and Rosettes are given

75

by the host club, and at the championship shows there are over 50 valuable trophies to be won annually, including the coveted Mendel Gold Cup for the best type. All these specials and cups are only available to members of the N.M.C.

The aim of every breeder is to obtain a championship strain. The N.M.C. recognizes a champion mouse as one that has won five first prizes in open competition under no less than three judges at three shows. Championships are doubled (ten first prizes), tripled and quadrupled until a mouse wins 25 first prizes and becomes the supreme champion. This noteworthy achievement is understandably only rarely attained, since the show career of a mouse is very short indeed.

There is little to be won in financial terms in the mouse fancy; even the consistent winners often only break even when prize money is compared to outlay. It is a fact that the mouse fancy has the lowest entry fee and prize money system of all the fancies, and perhaps herein lies the attraction. Mouse fanciers enjoy the thrill of competition and the sense of achievement and they experience from success on the show bench. This spirit engendered the saying, "A day at a show is a tonic."

12: Shows— How to Enter

Mouse shows are normally advertised in *F & F* or else duplicated schedules are sent out to members of the club organizing the event and to all known exhibitors. The advertisement will give the place and date of the forthcoming show, together with the names of the judges engaged and the show secretary's name and address to whom exhibitors are to send their entries. Sometimes the full list of classes is printed, otherwise a duplicated schedule will be sent on request.

On receiving the full schedule the exhibitor should consider which mice he wishes to enter and, once this has been decided, should complete his entry form and send it with the required fee to the show secretary at least a week before the show date. The secretary will then be able to fill out your entry and return your pen labels in time. The pen labels are the numbers given to each exhibit to assist the judge when placing the awards. They are glued on the reverse side and should be affixed to the left hand side of the Maxey cage. In this way the owner of each exhibit is anonymous, and fair play will always take place.

To guide the beginner, below is a fictitious sample classification of an N.M.C. supported show:

NMC Annual Cup Show sponsored by the London M.C. on Saturday, September 4th, 1976 at Show Hall,

77

Mouse Avenue, London. Judging commences at 10:30 a.m. Judges: Selfs: A. Goodman, Tans: A. Tanner, Marked: A. Markman, Satins and AOV: A. Topman.

Classes:
- 1. P.E. White Ad.
- 2. P.E. White U/8
- 3. Black/Blue Ad.
- 4. Black/Blue U/8
- 5. Cham/Fawn Ad.
- 6. Cham/Fawn U/8
- 7. A.O.C. Ad.
- 8. A.O.C. U/8
- d. 9. Self Chall. Ad.
- d. 10. Self Chall. U/8
- 11. Black/Choc Tan Ad.
- 12. Black/Choc Tan U/8
- 13. Cham/Silver Tan Ad.
- 14. Cham/Silver Tan U/8
- 15. Blue Tan A.A.
- 16. A.O.C. Tan Ad.
- 17. A.O.C. Tan U/8
- d. 18. Tan Chall. Ad.
- d. 19. Tan Chall. U/8
- 20. Dutch Ad.
- 21. Dutch U/8
- 22. Even/Broken Ad.
- 23. Even/Broken U/8
- 24. A.O.V. Marked Ad.
- 25. A.O.V. Marked U/8
- d. 26. Marked Chall. Ad.
- d. 27. Marked Chall. U/8
- 28. Satin Self Ad.
- 29. Satin Self U/8
- 30. Satin A.O.V. Ad.

     31. Satin A.O.V. U/8
d. 32. Satin Chall. Ad.
d. 33. Satin Chall. U/8
     34. Agouti/Cinn Ad.
     35. Agouti/Cinn U/8
     36. Chin/Fox Ad.
     37. Chin/Fox U/8
     38. Argente/Argente Creme Ad.
     39. Argente/Argente Creme U/8
     40. Longhaired A.A.
     41. A.O.V. Ad.
     42. A.O.V. U/8
d. 43. A.O.V. Chall. Ad.
d. 44. A.O.V. Chall. U/8
d. 45. Stud Buck
d. 46. Brood Doe
d. 47. Juv. A.V.A.A.
d. 48. Novice A.V.A.A.
d. 49. Ladies A.V.A.A.
d. 50. Pairs A.V.A.A.
d. 51. Doe Ad.
d. 52. Doe U/8
d. 53. Breeders Ad.
d. 54. Breeders U/8
d. 55. Grand Chall. Ad.
d. 56. Grand Chall. U/8
d. 57. Supreme Chall. A.V.A.A.
     d = must be duplicated

It can be seen that the schedule for all N.M.C. shows is divided into five sections, namely: Selfs, Tans, Marked, Satins and A.O.V. (Any Other Variety). Whether or not a judge is engaged for one or more sections, he is obliged to put forward the best from each section, example: five mice, and from these the Best in

Show is chosen. A Best in Show judge might be especially engaged for this purpose.

The abbreviations used in classifications and show reports could be rather confusing for beginners at first, so below is a list of these abbreviations and the terms generally used:

P.E.: Pink Eye
B.E.: Black Eye
Ad.: Adult
U/8: Under eight weeks of age
A.A.: Any age
A.O.C.: Any other color not previously specified
A.O.V.: Any other variety not previously specified
A.V.A.A.: Any variety, any age
Chall.: Challenge
Choc.: Chocolate
Cham.: Champagne
Cinn.: Cinnamon
Chin.: Chinchilla

d.: must be duplicated from the straight class. For example, the exhibit must be entered in class 1 before it can be entered in class nine or 55.

Stud Buck, Brood Doe: These classes are not judged by the standard, but rather as to how well the progeny can be envisaged. Thus the judge will require a heavy boned, masculine buck and a doe that looks as though she would raise a litter successfully.

Juv.: This class is restricted to juveniles.

Novice: A class for any exhibitor who has not won a first prize at a N.M.C. show.

Ladies: Lady exhibitors only.

Pairs: Two mice, in two Maxies. Both mice to be of the same variety and to be as much alike as possible; either sex allowed.

Doe: Judged to normal standard.

Breeders: Exhibit must have been bred by owner.

Grand and Supreme Chall.: Open to all mice.

Let us assume that the exhibitor has the following six mice he wishes to exhibit at this particular show: a P.E.W. U/8 weeks doe, a Self Silver buck, a Blue Tan adult doe, a Cream doe adult, an Agouti adult doe and a Silver Grey U/8 buck. An entry form may be sent to you by the show secretary but if not an entry can easily be made on a piece of ruled paper as set out below. The straight class is on the left, a description of the mouse comes next, followed by a list of the duplicate classes in which each mouse is to be entered and finally the total fee for each mouse is listed (assuming an entry fee of 5p per class). Do not forget to leave a blank space to the far right of the entry form, as this is for the show secretary to fill in the allotted pen number.

Makeshift entry form with the necessary information indicated.

Class	Variety	Duplicates						Fee	Pen No.
2	PEW U/8	10	48	52	54	56	57	.35	
7	BE Cream Ad.	9	48	51	53	55	57	.35	
7	Silver Buck	45	—	—	—	—	—	.10	
15	Blue Tan Ad.	18	48	—	—	55	—	.20	
34	Agouti Ad.	43	48	51	—	55	57	.30	
42	Silver Grey U/8	—	—	—	—	—	—	.05	
								£1.35	

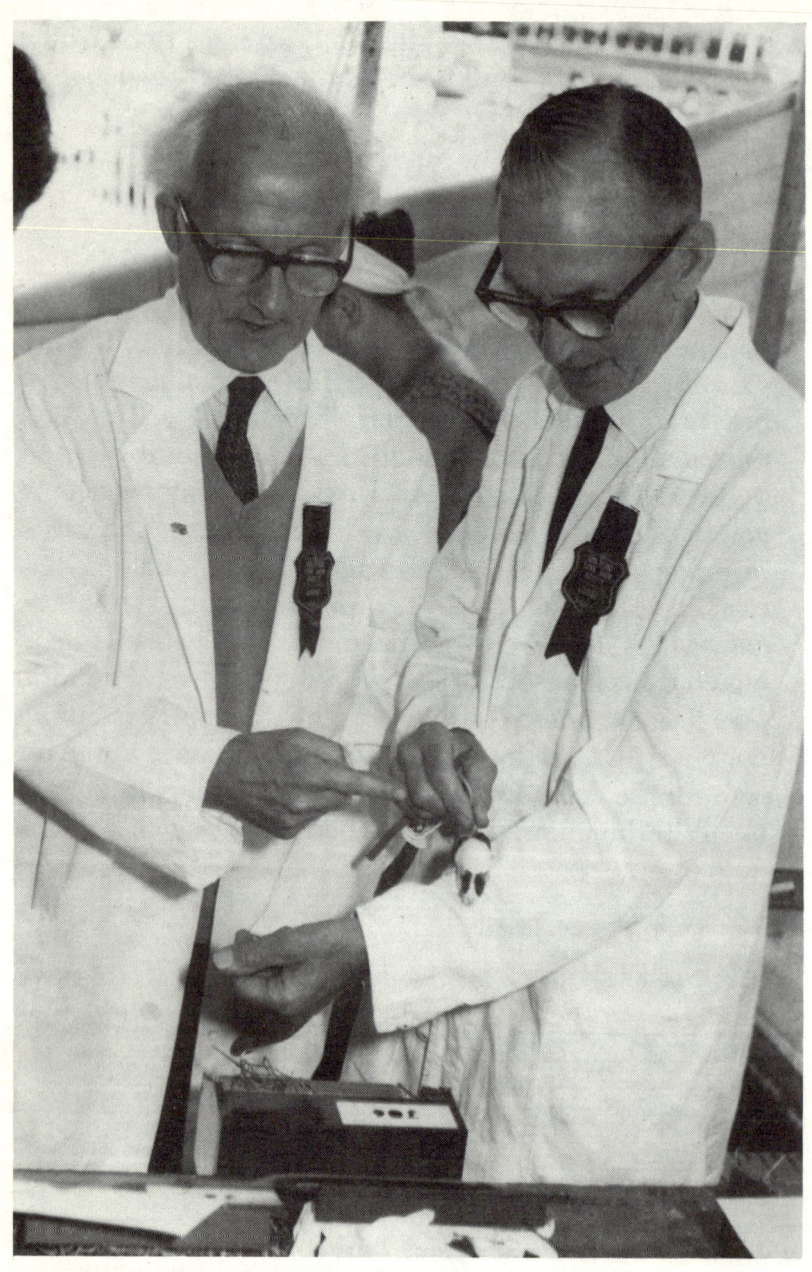

Two judges in the process of discussing the qualifications of a Dutch Mouse.

Of the assumed six mice, the exhibitor has decided that the young White, the adult Cream and the golden Agouti are his best chances, and therefore they have been entered in the most classes. The White and the Cream have been entered throughout, because they have both been bred by our novice exhibitor. The Agouti has been purchased from a breeder and therefore cannot be entered in class 53.

The self buck has been entered specifically for the stud buck class since, although he is a fine specimen, large and typical, he has not the condition and finish required to compete with good quality does in the duplicates. He must however be entered in his straight class (No. 7).

Although the Blue Tan is an adult, he can compete against youngsters in the straight class, which can be entered by mice of any age, before going forward to challenge the tan adult (class 18).

The Silver Grey U/8 weeks is not a particularly good specimen and is only entered in one class to see how it fares. Although it is a buck, it would not be entered in the stud buck class because the judge would not consider a young mouse as being ready for stud purposes.

If the exhibitor is attending the show himself, he could tell the show secretary and then obtain his pen labels at the show rather than have them sent by return post. If, however, he is not attending and is sending stock by rail, he should ask that a rail label and pen labels be forwarded. The rail label will already be addressed to the location of the show; all the exhibitor has to do is write his own name and address on the return label which is underneath and attach the label to the travelling box. It is advisable to pin a copy of your entry form (with the pen number added) together with your name and address to the inside lid of your travelling

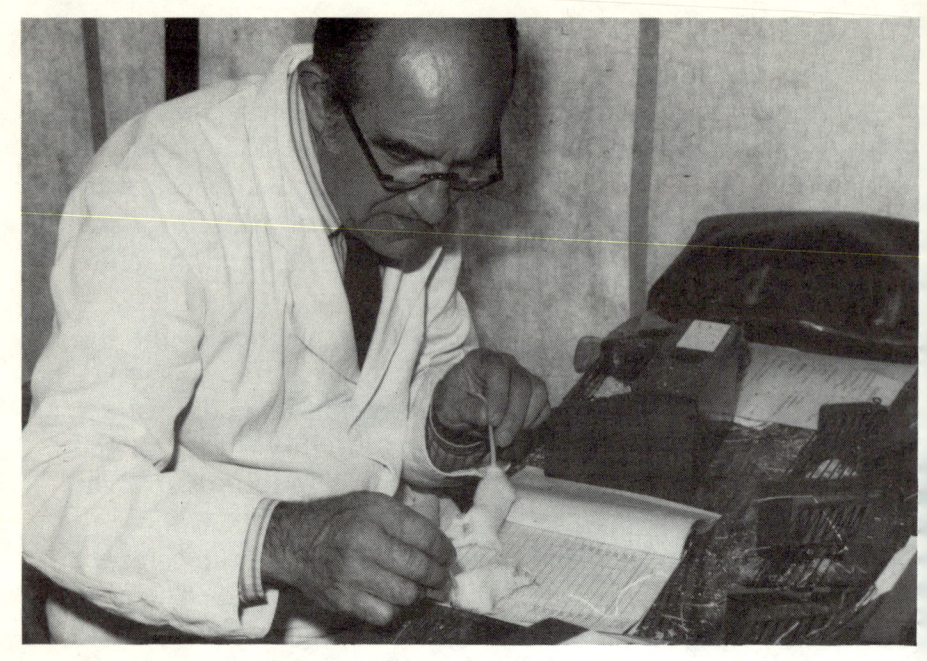

This judge is giving a pair of mice a final check prior to recording his evaluation.

box. This will greatly assist the stewards who unpack and then replace your Maxies and also guards against any mistakes being made.

If sending stock to the show by rail, the box should be sent at least 24 hours before the show day. However, it is advisable to ship by Thursday night for a Saturday show in order to ensure safe arrival in time for judging. The mice will be in fine condition, so there is not need to worry (see Show Preparation). Expect the stock to return the day after the show, and if you wish to collect the mice yourself from your local railway station, indicate this on your rail label with the name of your local station and the initials "T.B.C.F." (To Be Called For). A telephone number will also help as the station master will then phone you as soon as the stock has arrived.

13: Show Preparation

No special preparations are required for showing fancy mice. In fact, the majority of fanciers take their exhibition stock straight out of the boxes, into the Maxies and onto the show bench. This is yet another advantage of breeding mice for exhibition in comparison with some other fancies where the animals require endless hours of grooming, cleaning and washing before being ready for competition.

Some exhibitors believe in gently rubbing their mice with a piece of silk cloth for about a week before the show to help the shine of the coat. However, I believe that even this is unnecessary, for mice are very clean creatures and groom themselves in much the same way as their natural enemy the cat would do. They have, as do all fur-coated animals, a natural oil in the coat which gives a lovely sheen or bloom when in full coat and good condition. Indeed, it is not advisable to over-handle exhibition stock just before a show or the natural sheen may be spoiled. It should go without saying that the fancier's hands should always be clean before handling stock, whether for exhibition or not, to prevent any dirt from being transferred to the animal.

Although show preparation as such is not required, show condition is all-important and often means the difference between first and second place. Condition must first be bred for and then maintained by good management. A short, sleek coat sparkles beautifully when in good condition, so all hairy, long-coated specimens must be discarded from breeding operations. No living creature can maintain 100 percent top condition forever and fancy mice, which are small creatures with correspondingly small stomachs, can lose condition easily. It is the job of the conscientious and careful exhibitor to help his stock reach top condition on the day of the show, no sooner or later. The judges' phrase "shown to the minute" then takes on full meaning.

Every fancier gives his exhibition stock that little extra conditioning food for about two weeks before the show. Some will place all their possibles together in a box filled with fresh hay so that they can work through the hay, make tunnels, search for food and generally

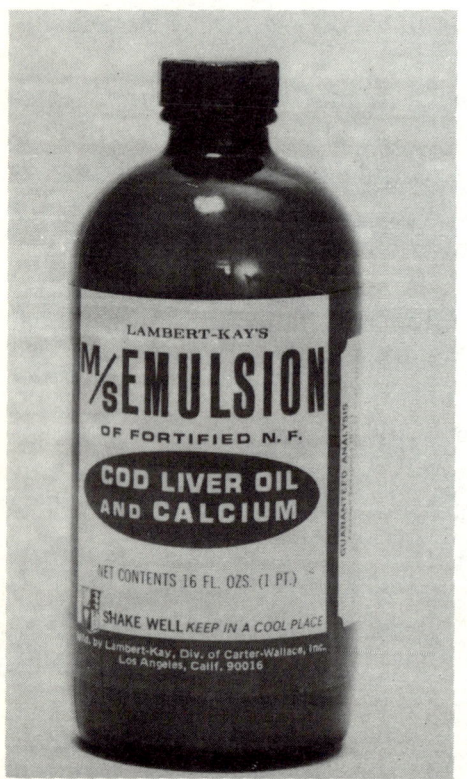

Cod liver oil is a good source of vitamin A and is also a well known coat conditioner. Dietary supplements and conditioners are available at all pet shops carrying supplies for rodent pets.

keep active, thereby attaining tip-top condition. Sunflower seeds and white millet are excellent conditioners and can be given on alternate days in addition to the normal diet of clipped oats and bread mash. A little raw linseed oil mixed with the bread and milk about three times per week will greatly enhance the natural oil in the coat. Care must be taken not to overdo such a mixture; otherwise the coat will appear greasy. Some fanciers prefer raw eggs instead of linseed and such a mash is certainly appreciated by the mice. Linseed can also be given in seed form, although I have found this method to be very wasteful.

Keep an eye on the stock the last few days before the show to ensure that not too much mash is being given, or the mice might become slightly plump. In any case, gradually cut down the mash and do not feed any mash at all the night before the show. Moisture can be given in the form of a little green, carrot or potato. With some experience, the novice will soon be able to gauge the amount of food required for conditioning for shows. The one problem that cannot be solved is molt. Mice can begin to molt very quickly and without warning. A mouse with serious molt will never win in decent competition, so it is a waste of time to exhibit an animal that is in two coats. If the animal has started to molt, the process can be speeded up by feeding boiled linseed regularly, so the mouse may have molted through in time for the show. However, it may be as well to wait until the full coat is through when the animal can be shown at its best.

Since the mouse spends its whole exhibition career in the Maxey cage, these should be properly looked after. The Maxies should be kept clean and dry and special attention should be given to the wired fronts. These could go rusty from dampness or condensation, and could easily spoil a good exhibition animal, because the mice have a habit of chewing the bars, in which case the nose would easily become stained. Such a rust mark would soon put the mouse down in the awards, so it is worthwhile to periodically clean and repaint the bars of the cages.

Sawdust should be placed in the Maxies, together with hay or paper shavings. There should be sufficient hay to make the exhibit warm and comfortable on its journey. Too much may cause the mouse to overheat and sweat, perhaps even molt; too little will not afford the mouse protection against the weather. In either case the chance of success will be minimized. A little seed should also be placed in the cage (no pots etc. allowed). Some oats, sunflower and dog biscuit would suffice, together with a small piece of carrot for moisture, but no wet food should be given as it may ruin the coat. If showing delicate shades, such as whites, then carrot may possibly stain, so give raw potato instead. If sending stock by rail give the stock enough seeds to last for a couple of days at least and they will be in perfect condition on arrival. For long journeys in winter, I prefer Maxies with lids because they provide more warmth for the mice.

I have seen Maxies at many shows containing very little hay or food and consequently the mice are huddled in a corner, with coats standing on end, looking very pathetic indeed. Needless to say these mice won nothing, whereas a little effort would have given the animals a fair chance.

A chapter on show preparation would perhaps not be complete without a word on washing mice, with special reference to P.E. Whites. All animals could benefit to some degree if washed before exhibition, for the coats could contain a certain amount of dirt from the breeder's hands, dirty hay, etc. However, unless you are exhibiting whites, there is really no cause for

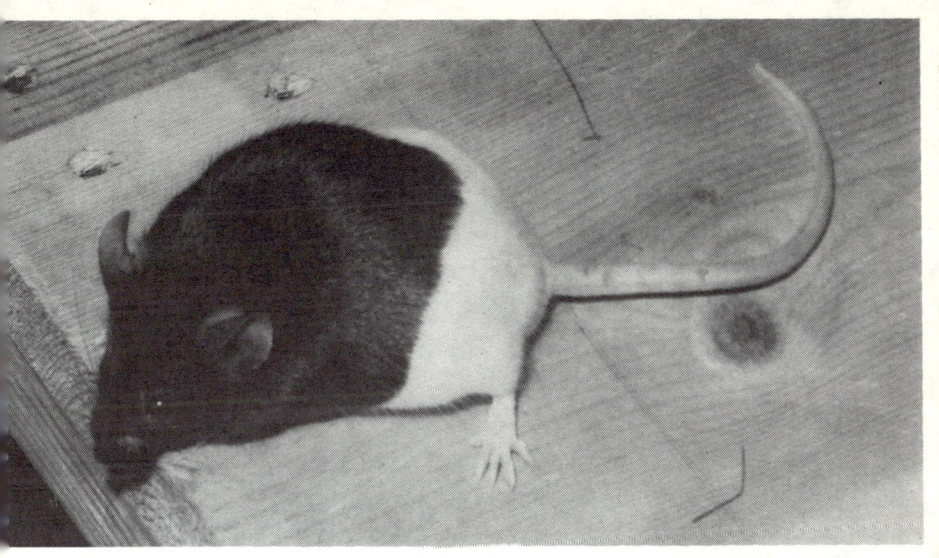

In addition to possessing the requirements for a particular mouse category, each entrant must have the basic ideal mouse appearance of good health and proportions. This White Rump Mouse is too fat.

A judge looking over each data sheet of the many entries to the show for his evaluation.

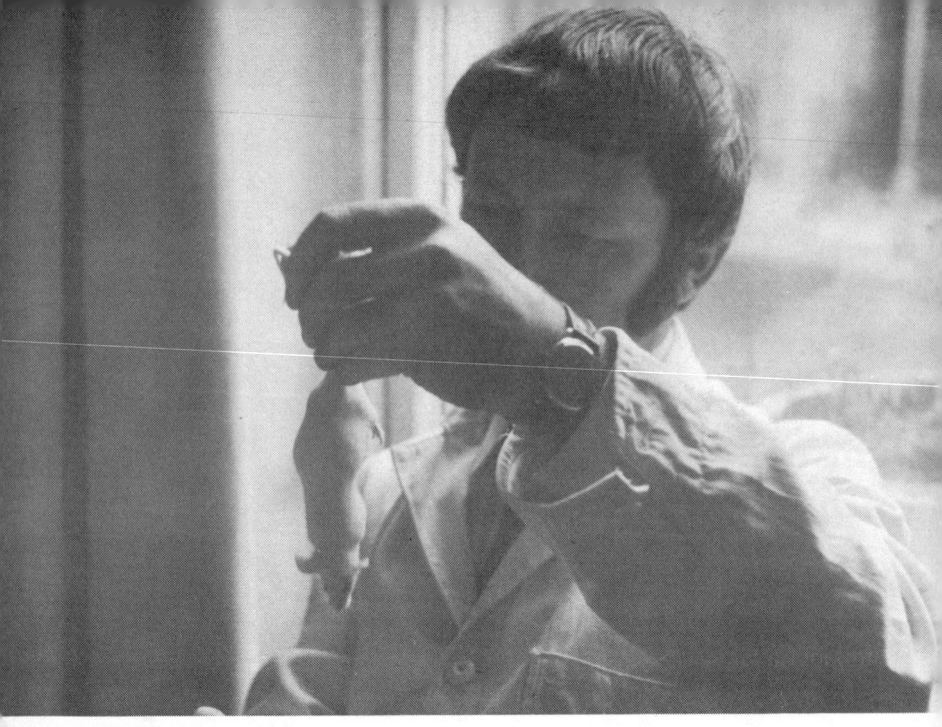

If held properly, as demonstrated by this judge, a mouse will not be in any distress at all.

Regardless of the place, an unconfined and unattended mouse will certainly go astray.

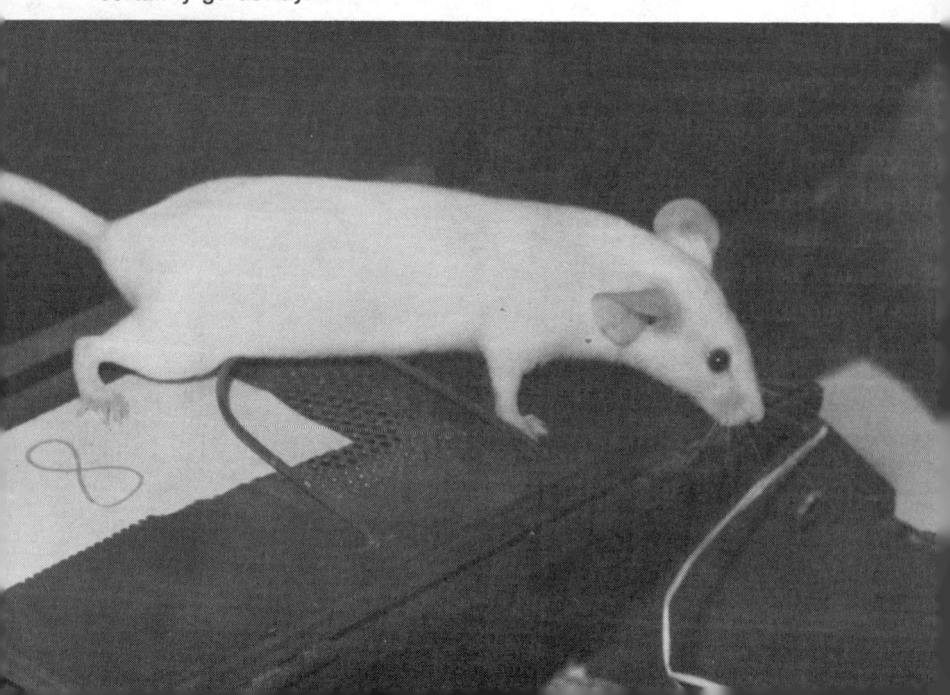

The author and Dan Holland of the London and Southern Counties Mouse Club weighing the qualifications of an entry to the show.

washing mice. To win in top class competition with P.E. Whites it is undoubtedly necessary to wash and powder the exhibit. Many fanciers frown upon the use of powder, but my own experience recommends its use, and it is certainly used on other white exhibition animals such as rabbits, cavies and dogs. Apart from powdering, any other form of artificial aid is illegal, and could result in serious consequences if discovered.

Preparing whites for exhibition involves a great deal of patience and should not be attempted by the novice. The specialist in whites must keep his stock scrupulously clean at all times. The boxes must be spotless and clean vegetable and parchment paper shav-

91

ings should be used, because hay contains dust and dirt. The mouse should be placed on a suitable surface and washed all over with an old shaving brush or piece of cotton wool in slightly warmed distilled water with a little powdered soap or a good shampoo added. Do not use a detergent powder as this will ruin the mouse's coat. Firmly hold the mouse by the root of the tail to wash the top of the mouse, but do not touch the bottom because the belly fur is too thin to be washed. Stage two requires another small bowl of warm water with pure vinegar added, which neutralizes the action of the soap or shampoo. Finally, rinse the mouse in clear, warm water and dry with a soft towel. Put the mouse in a clean Maxey, fill the cage with paper shavings, then place it near the fire so the mouse can dry. When dry, say after about an hour, place the mouse in a small cardboard box filled to a depth of about one inch with talcum powder or corn starch. Rub the powder into the coat with a soft dry brush and then replace the mouse in a perfectly clean box in the shed. Repeat the powdering process until three days before the show. Clean out the breeding box and change the bedding. Gently rub down the mouse with a silk cloth to remove any surplus powder; this will put a gloss on the coat. The mouse is then ready for the show.

14: Stewarding—Means to an End

The greatest single problem for novices who begin exhibiting is which mice to exhibit and which to leave at home. There is no simple answer to this problem, and the best way to acquire knowledge here, as with anything else, is to learn by experience. If you are fortunate enough to have an experienced fancier friend living nearby, he will no doubt help you choose the most suitable mice for exhibition until you are confident that you can spot a winner yourself.

Certainly there is no substitute for actually going to the shows, whether exhibiting or not. Speak to fanciers at the shows, ask questions, listen and learn. Compare the winners of each class with the also-rans. The main difference may be one of fitness, but if there is no discernable difference, ask someone to point out why one beat the other. It may be a question of better type, larger ears, etc., or it may be that a slight difference in color was the deciding factor. Every person sees color in a different way, and thus we may have slightly different winners under different judges. Type, size, ears, etc., are constant throughout all varieties, but color is very difficult to describe. The only way to fix in your mind's eye exactly what constitutes the correct color is to attend shows and see the winners. Make a special pont of examining the Best in Show mouse and the best of each section, (e.g., Best Self, Tan, etc.). These animals should be fine examples of their respective breeds, and your aim should be to surpass them!

Possibly the best way to gain experience is to volunteer to be a steward. Stewarding can be a means to an end for the novice, for not only will he become an active, helpful part of the show, but he will be learning all the time he is doing his job. Being a good steward is not a difficult task; basically, all that is required of him is to place before the judge each class in turn as requested. The hay should be taken out and placed behind each Maxey so that the judge can easily remove the exhibits. The hay can then be returned to its original cage, which I believe is only proper. At some shows, stewards place the hay in a pile until after the class is judged, and then anybody's hay is placed in the Maxey. If a fancier has taken the trouble to prepare his Maxey with good dry soft hay, it seems unfair to me that it would be replaced after only one class with hay that might be damp, stalky or flea-ridden. The chances of the mouse may well be damaged in the challenge classes later on.

If you explain to the judge that you are a novice and that you would be grateful if he could comment on the mice for your benefit, I am sure he would oblige once he has finished judging. In this way you will learn of the faults to look for in each variety and you will discover if the judge leans this way or that on certain faults or good points. When you exhibit under the judge in the future you will know what he prefers and can enter mice accordingly.

One word of warning, however: Never pass comments on the mice yourself whether or not you are stewarding. A good judge will never be influenced by comments in any case, but they are in bad taste and are much frowned upon in any fancy. When judging has been completed you are then quite at liberty to ask the judge his opinion of your own mice, and I advise you

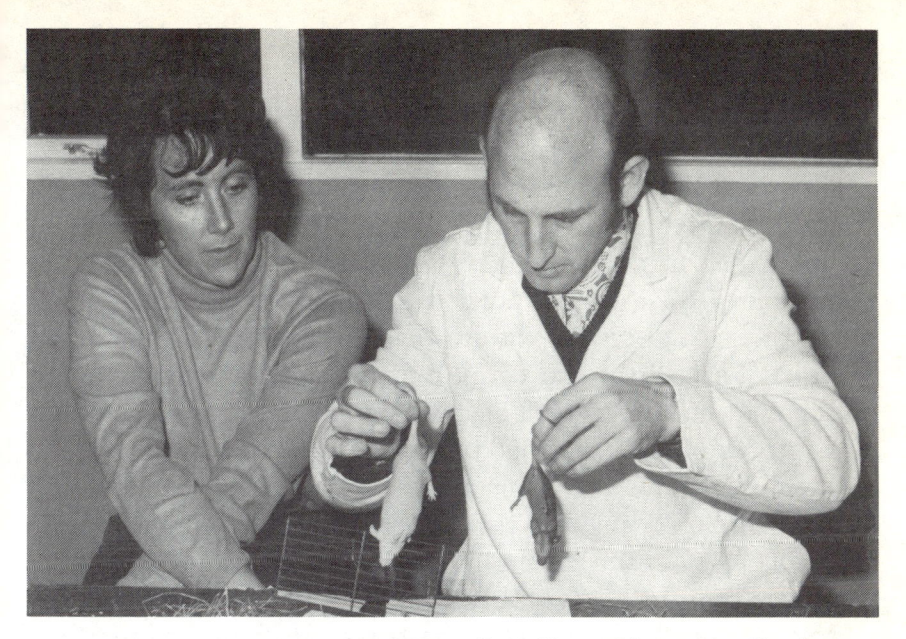

Mouse judge Tony Cooke of Petersfield, Hampshire making the decision while his wife Gillian watches closely in anticipation.

During a mouse show, hay, in particular, gets so shuffled about that the help of an assistant or steward will really be appreciated by any participant.

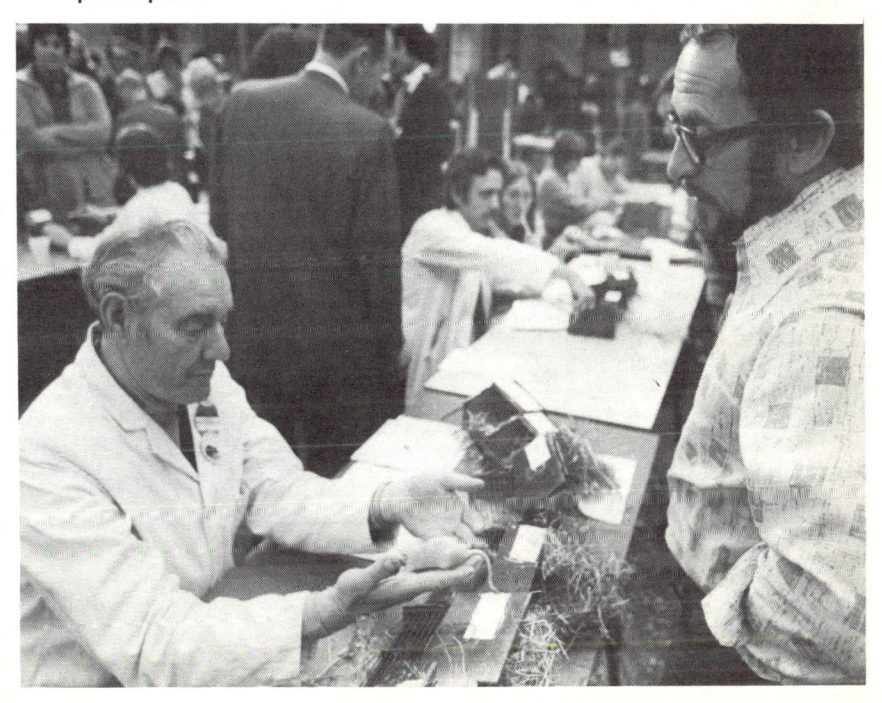

very much to do so. If you are unaware of the particular shade of color, etc., that a judge believes fits the standard, then enter two or three mice of different shades, a light, a medium and a dark shade. You will soon find out which is best. Whatever the color, only enter mice that are fit, in good condition and free from molt.

The final task of the steward is to collect the stock of each exhibitor who was not at the show and prepare them to be returned. The mice must be fed with oats and bread mash (supplied by the Club) and replaced in their respective travelling boxes. Make sure they have sufficient bedding for they may have a long journey before they reach home. When replacing the Maxies, ensure that the backs rather than the wire fronts are facing the ventilation holes of the travelling boxes, to prevent any direct draft on the mice. Finally, sign the contents label, so as to indicate that you have tended the stock as well as you would have liked your stock attended by someone else.

To sum up, study the standards, go to the shows and, most important, never be afraid to ask. The more questions you ask, the more answers you will receive and the more you will learn.

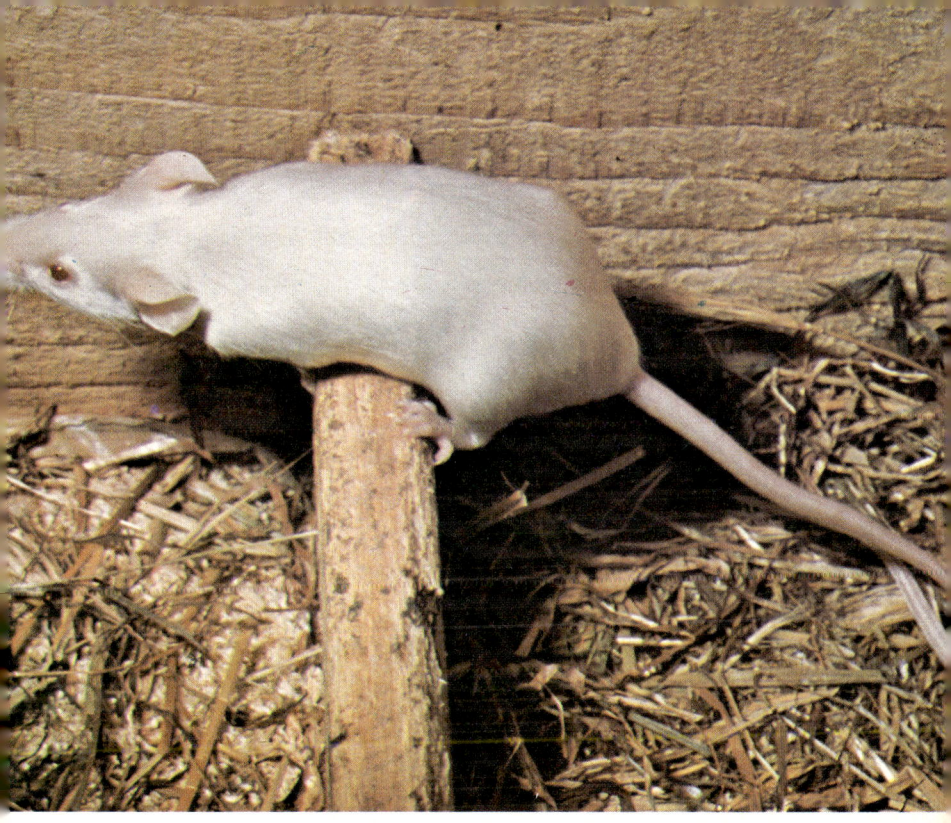

An Ivory Satin mouse. Ivory is synonymous to white in Satins.

15: The Standard of Excellence

Written standards are necessarily deficient, for words cannot convey an exact idea of what any mouse should look like. This inadequacy applies particularly to the definition of color. It is for this reason that attendance at shows is urged upon all who wish to form an accurate picture of the varieties of fancy mice, for nothing can adequately take the place of first hand inspection of good specimens.

Notwithstanding the above, the standards as laid down by the N.M.C. give as concise a definition as possible in the written word. Below is the General Standard of Excellence as adopted by the N.M.C., which has changed little since the club was founded: "The Mouse must be long in body with long clean head, not too fine or pointed at the nose. The eyes should be large, bold and prominent. The ears large and tulip shaped, free from creases, carried erect with plenty of width between them. The body should be long and slim, a trifle arched over the loin, and racy in appearance. The tail, which must be free from kinks, should come well out of the back, and be thick at the root or set-on, gradually tapering like a whip-lash to a fine end, the length being about equal to that of the Mouse's body. The coat should be short, perfectly smooth, glossy and sleek to the hand. The Mouse should be perfectly tractable, free from any vice, and not subject to fits or other similar ailments. Sunken eyes, kinked tails, or fits to lose 20 points. A mouse without whiskers shall be disqualified."

It should be emphasized that although there are over 50 different varieties of fancy mice, there is but one general standard or ideal for size, type, ears, eyes and tail. This fact should certainly make breeding and judging easier, but in actual practice this is not always the case. There will always be some variance between individuals of most strains due to genetic variability and environmental differences in breeding and rearing techniques.

The ideal type as above is of course somewhat different depending upon sex. A genuine masculine buck would never be able to compete with a doe in shape and carriage. A decent stud buck should have a heavier bone structure than a doe. Its coat tends to be coarser and does not show condition as well as the soft, short coat of the doe. Indeed, if a buck could be mistaken for a doe, he should not be used for stud purposes, for his progeny will be much too fine in bone, with narrow skulls and thin tails. Although the majority of the red cards at the shows go to the female of the species, bucks do win regularly in certain varieties where markings and color are of utmost importance, for example Dutch and Broken Marked. Yet because bucks generally cannot compete with does, stud buck classes have been initiated, and it is certainly an honor to win in this highly competitive class.

For practical reasons fancy mice have been divided into separate groups to facilitate judging. These classifications are:

1. Selfs: Mice of one color only.
2. Tans: Of any recognized top color with tan belly color.
3. Marked: Piebald markings.
4. Satins: Any color or markings but with satinized coat.
5. A.O.V.: Any other variety not classified in the previous sections, example: ticked or shaded coloring.

16: The Selfs

Selfs are recognized in the following colors: white, black, blue, chocolate, cream, champagne, silver, dove, red and fawn. Three colors, whites, creams and silvers, are recognized with both black or pink eyes. The N.M.C. Standard states: "The color should be carried evenly throughout the whole body and should extend to the skin. Ears, nails, tail and belly should be of the same color, and the color should be solid from tip of nose to set-on of tail."

Two Self Doves are seen here being compared to each other.

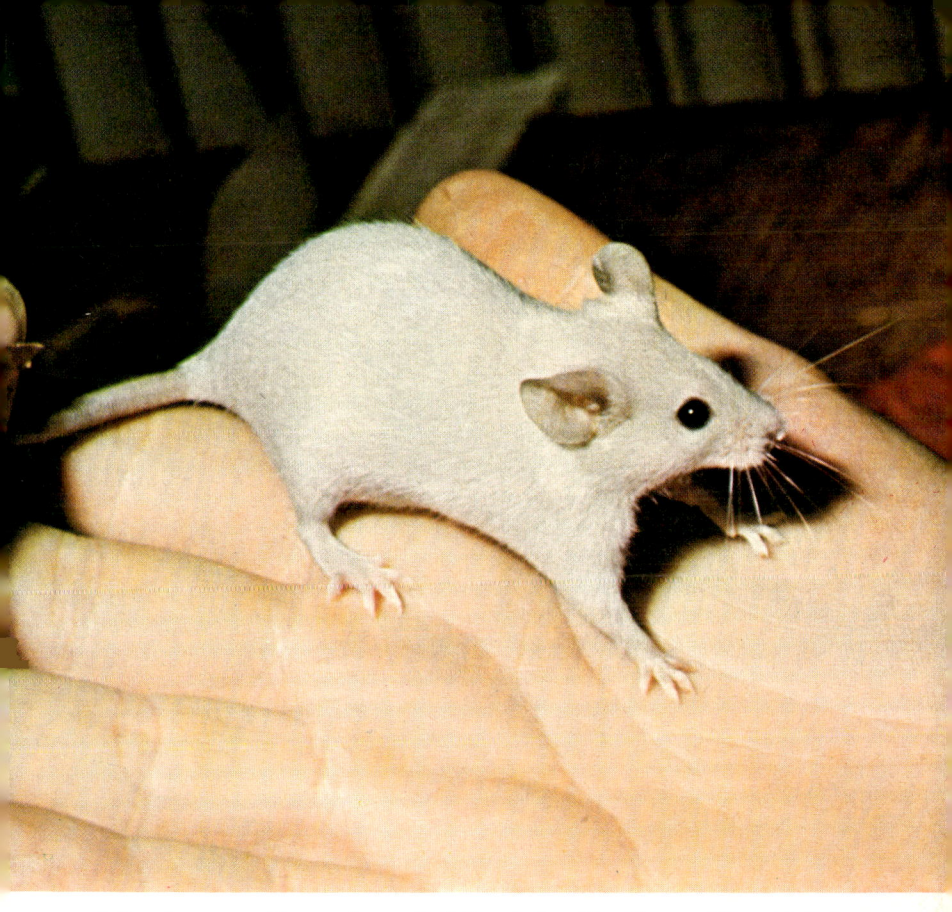

A Pearl mouse. The undercoat of Pearls is pale silver, with each hair tipped with gray or black.

POINTS FOR THE SELF VARIETIES

Color	50
Condition—not fat, short and glossy coat	15
Shape and carriage	10
Size	5
Ears—shape, size and position	5
Eyes—large, bold and prominent	5
Muzzle—long, strength carried out to an end	5
Tail—long and uniform, no kinks	5
	100

It can be seen from the standard just how important color is in the Selfs, but it should be remembered

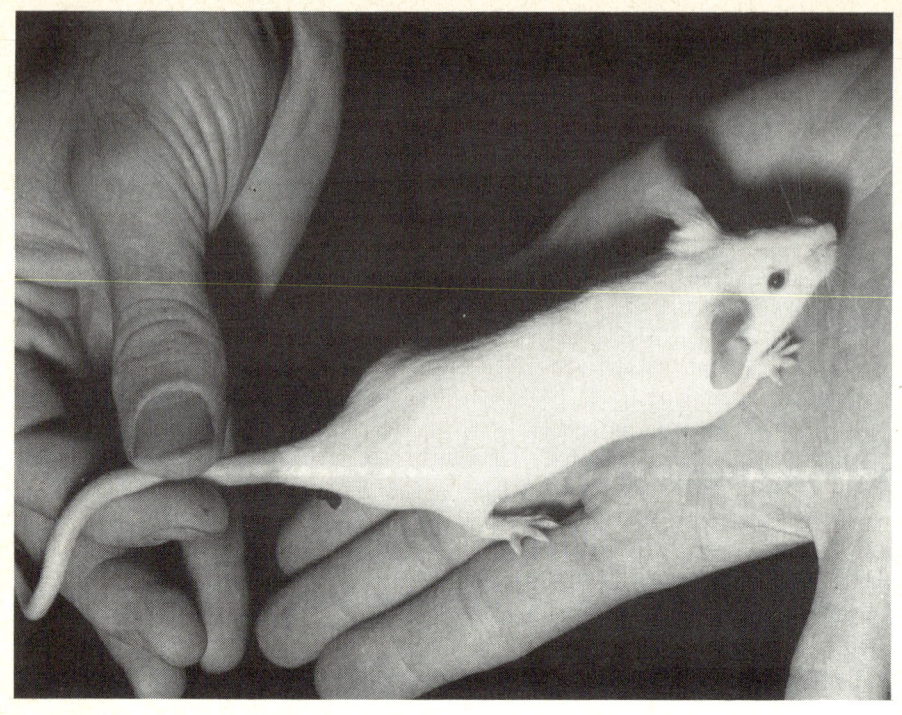

A Black-Eyed Cream, one of the recognized Selfs.

that without good size, type and minor points a mouse will not go very far in the exhibition world. I would say that the Selfs, of all varieties, generally come closest to the ideal with respect to color and type. Perhaps it is because breeders have only had to concentrate on one color that they have been able to cultivate the Selfs to such a high standard, whereas the Tan and Marked breeders have had to consider variable factors in their breeding operations. The Selfs also are some of the oldest varieties in existence, and thus have been brought nearer to perfection over the years. However, it should be realized that the N.M.C. Standards do not award points for difficulty in breeding any variety. Sometimes it will be more difficult to win a good quality class of Selfs than to win a class of, say, only average Tans. Yet there is a saying in the fancy that "a good one of any variety will always win," and that certainly is true.

The main difficulty in breeding Selfs is to perfect the evenness of color as required in the standard. This is particularly true of belly color, which is usually lighter than the top. The basic reason for this is that the fur of the belly is not so dense as the top, which would undoubtedly make for a lighter shade of color. This slight fault is well known by breeders and judges alike and some allowances should be made. Obviously, when selecting matings all mice with thin belly fur should be discarded if at all possible.

Generally speaking, the Selfs can be recommended for the new fancier provided he obtains good foundation stock from a winning strain and keeps to that strain only. It should not be assumed that all the ten colors of Self are equal with respect to size, type, etc., for various factors influence these points as will be described below.

P.E. WHITES

In days past the Pink-Eyed White was the pinnacle of the fancy mouse. The variety had many followers and excelled in size, type and minor points such as large ears, bold eyes and strong tail. Because of its value as an outcross, most fanciers carried a few P.E. Whites if only for experimentation and for improving other varieties kept.

Today the position of the P.E.W. as the most perfected mouse has been threatened by several varieties, notably the P.E. Silver, Champagne, B.E. Cream and the Argente. No longer is the White the largest and typiest mouse seen on the show bench, and indeed many say that the quality of the variety has deteriorated when compared to past winners. Certainly the P.E.W. rarely wins the premier awards at shows today, whereas once it was nearly always one of the top varieties at all the shows. Perhaps the reason for this is that modern judges are rather wary of the super China

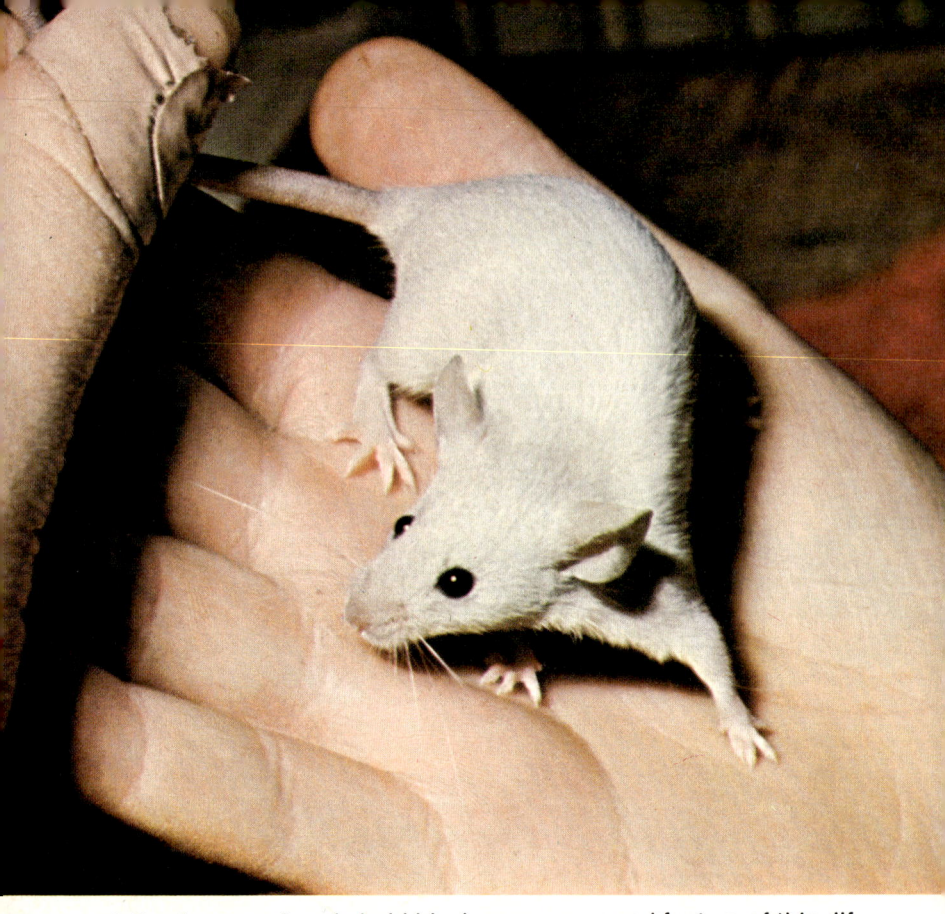

A Pearl mouse. Lovely bold black eyes are a good feature of this difficult variety.

Whites that appear from time to time on the show bench. There seems to be a strong feeling in the fancy today that powdering of Whites is a bad practice, yet it is accepted in other fancies. It is up to the individual to make his own decision on this rather delicate subject. Although Whites can be shown in the young classes without washing or powdering, certainly the variety is not for the beginner; when molted into an adult coat a slight yellow tinge does appear, especially along the flanks. The beginner often chooses P.E.W. for exhibiting with on the grounds that a White is a White only and will not be as confusing as some of the other varieties appear to be. But, I would ask, can the begin-

A Silver-Tan mouse. The contrast between the tan belly and the silver coat is not as dramatic as in the Black and Tan or any other dark coat.

ner realistically hope to compete with those experienced exhibitors of Whites who practice show preparation? In any case there are shades of white, some mice being whiter than others. The N.M.C. Standard asks for Whites to be pure in color, and this has to be selectively bred for, whether or not show preparation is to be practiced.

P.E. Whites, if of outstanding size and type, etc., and if used correctly, can be very valuable as an outcross for many varieties. In albinos the color make-up is not expressed in the coat because a genetic factor for color development is absent. Albinos will only produce albinos, but when crossed to a colored mouse its hidden potential will become apparent in most of the progeny. It is a grave mistake to assume that because an albino is white it will lighten the color of any cross-matings. Actually, the reverse may happen if P.E.W.s of the wrong genetic makeup are used. Theoretically there are as many kinds of P.E. White as there are colored forms of fancy mouse. Probably the best P.E. Whites are those carrying P.E. Silver genetically, and breeders often keep these varieties as one strain.

BLACK-EYED WHITES

The B.E.W. is as far removed from the P.E.W. as is imaginable. Whereas the P.E.W. is an albino, the B.E.W. is a pied mouse devoid of markings, except for the eye which is obviously pigmented. The so-called pink eye is not colored as such, for what we are seeing are the blood vessels behind the transparent eye. B.E.W.s are extremely difficult to breed and are far inferior to P.E.W.s in size and type. Genetically, B.E.W.s are closely related to another difficult variety, the Variegated, and both these varieties are near extinction, although one or two fanciers are making valiant efforts to reintroduce them to the fancy. A large proportion of marked specimens turn up in the litters of B.E.W., and the lightest marked does should be mated to the purest colored buck in the hope that a fair percentage of clear Whites turn up.

THE BLACK
"The color should be a dense lustrous black. Eye Black"

Top class Self Blacks are beautiful exhibition animals, since the color black seems to reflect good conditions better than any other color. Self Black mice are very popular and it would be well worthwhile for the beginner to consider them. Competition is keen because the Black has been so cultivated that no odd alien hairs are accepted on the show bench, even including the toenails, which must all be black to match the rest of the animal. Often we see in show reports "loses on feet," which means that the mouse in question was equal to the winner except that its feet were light or had white

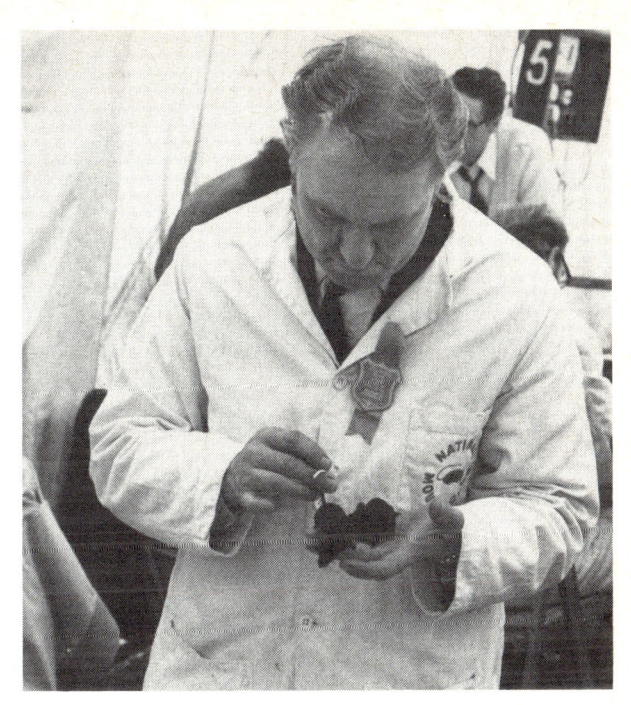

Mouse judge Jack Hartley of Manchester is inspecting two black mice.

toenails. Therefore, it is important to select for this point in breeding operations. Also, any mice with an odd white hair or two in the coat should be discarded or this fault probably will re-occur.

A prevalent fault with Blacks is the occurrence of tan hairs around the vent and below the throat. It should seem natural that tan hairs predominate around these areas, but it is something that must be selectively bred out. It can be done with patience, but even so some of the very best Blacks will have a few tan hairs in these areas.

Color in Blacks is now near perfection, and to retain this quality Black to Black matings would seem to be best. Some breeders of Blacks will occasionally try an outcross of Self Black to improve size and type, points for which the Black is not noted. In fact, many fanciers keep both Blacks and Blues in their mousery, and each is crossed with the other when desired. A couple of the best Blue does should be mated to your best Black stud

107

buck. From the resultant litter, which will be entirely black, keep only does and mate these back to a Black buck. Feet will undoubtedly suffer for a couple of generations. In any case, keep the outcross separate until you are sure it is worthwhile, and only then introduce into the main stud. This last rule applies to all outcrosses and is really only common sense.

A more dramatic outcross to improve size and type in Blacks is to P.E. Whites carrying Silver or Dove. Never use Whites carrying Chocolate or Champagne or an undeniable rusty tinge will appear in the coats and is practically impossible to eradicate. If the beginner feels he really needs an outcross for his Self Blacks, I would

A Blue Tan mouse. The feet of this individual are good; the inside is tan and the top is of the same color as the rest of the body.

A close-up of a Black Tan buck showing the sharp demarcation between the top color and the tan belly.

seriously suggest he try a Black from another leading strain. This is by far the safest outcross to maintain color in Blacks. Because the black gene (or gene-complex) makes the pure Self Black mouse genetically smaller in bone structure than most other varieties, I feel that P.E. Whites should be considered for use as foster mothers. The specialists in Blacks could then ensure that maximum growth potential is attained.

THE BLUE
"The color should be medium slate blue. Eye Black"

The Blue is closely allied to the Black but is nowhere near as popular nor as cultivated. The Blue suffers from basically the same faults as its cousin; for example, the Blue has tan vents, white hairs, light feet, although it is potentially of better size and type. It is difficult with this variety to consistently produce the medium slate blue color as required by the standard. Light, medium and dark shades will appear in the litters, and they must be blended to produce the ideal. The blue dilution factor creates a distinctly ticked or clumping appearance in the lighter shades, which is most undesirable in the Self and should be guarded against. If the top color or the feet are becoming too light then the natural outcross is to a Self Black. Here again do not use Chocolate or the blue color will be ruined. As described above, mate some typey Blue does to a Black buck. Blacks and Blues will both be in the litter, but it is easy to distinguish the darker Blacks and cull them. Henceforth mate Blue to Blue and select for the best.

THE CHOCOLATE
"The color should be that of plain [not milk] chocolate and should be rich, deep and full of life. Eye Black"

The Chocolate is one of the Selfs that has few devotees, and it is rare indeed that this variety wins a mixed straight class, let alone Best Self. Few fanciers seem willing to take up this rather neglected breed, yet a good Self Chocolate is a beautiful exhibition animal. There is no reason why Chocolates of good size and type cannot be bred, for they do not have the retarding black genetic factor to hold them back in this respect. Like Blacks and Blues however, Chocolates suffer from tan vents and throat spots. In Chocolates this fault seems to be worse, perhaps because they are in few hands and

The auctioning of mice is one of the activities during an exhibit. This is an excellent opportunity of getting mice of known ancestry and good quality.

have not been cultivated. Often there are also tan hairs along the flanks and around the teats of does, faults that obviously put the Chocolate down in competition against other Selfs. The only safe outcross is to a soundly colored Black, which ensures that the color is kept dark. Since Black is dominant all the first generation will be Black and these mice should be either mated together or else to another Chocolate. From the subsequent litters the breeder must select only the very best for future matings.

Breeding of Chocolates is not difficult, although the would-be fancier will have a problem in finding good foundation stock. There is certainly an opportunity for someone to make a name for himself by revitalizing the Self Chocolate. It will require a lot of patience but it is not impossible.

111

THE CREAM

"The color should be a very pale cream, not to be confused with ivory, stone or very dilute champagne. Eye Pink or Black"

In the early days of the fancy the Cream was considered to be the most difficult of all the Selfs to produce satisfactorily. In those days it was a product of Red crossed with Blue, but the modern Cream has been produced by chinchillating the Self Chocolate. The result is an extremely fine mouse indeed, so much so, in fact that the B.E. Cream has superseded the P.E.W. as the "ideal" fancy mouse.

A Black Tan mouse. Tans are popular, and they occur in many varieties. Note the rich golden tan color of this specimen's belly.

Shown here is a winning Argente Creme which became an N.M.C. champion.

The Cream can be recommended to the beginner, although competition is very strong from established studs. Size and type are superb on the B.E. Cream, and any mice failing on these points should be discarded. Strong tail and set-on, large bat-like ears and big bold eyes are also features of this variety. The P.E.W. can at all times be used as a first cross to the B.E. Cream and winners could immediately result from such a cross. However, any P.E. babies from this cross should definitely *not* be used for breeding Pink-Eyed Whites; otherwise the Whites will be utterly ruined. Such pink-eyed babies can, however, be shown in the under eight weeks white class, but after this age they develop a yellow tinge and are only suitable for further cream breeding. Pink-Eyed Creams are rarely, if ever, exhibited.

The White cross should not be resorted to very often or belly color will suffer and become far too light. The best P.E.W.s to use are those that have been Silver bred.

Many dark shades of beige or lilac crop up in Cream breeding and it is important not to destroy all of them. Constant breeding together of the winning shade of cream will eventually lead to mice not cream but dirty white. Thus the lilac shades should be retained at all times and mated to lighter shades to produce that ideal pale cream as required in the standard.

THE CHAMPAGNE
"The color should be that of champagne silk with a pinkish tinge, free from mealiness and well carried out under. Eye Pink"

The Self Champagne is a very attractive color and is one of the most popular of all the varieties of fancy mice. The variety has much to recommend itself and beginners who have chosen the Champagne have often won the highest awards when first starting to exhibit them. Genetically the Champagne is a Pink-Eyed Chocolate, that is to say it is a Chocolate carrying a double dose of the pink-eyed dilution factor which turns the coat color from chocolate to champagne.

Since its color is very difficult to describe, the Self Champagne is one of the varieties that should be studied at the shows. Once seen, however, the correct color is never forgotten. Various shades have to be used in the breeding to achieve the desired delicate shade with a pink tinge to it. Breeders blend light, medium and dark shades, and any super light or pale shades should be discarded along with the very dark or muddy shades.

A young fellow getting acquainted with a new friend.

P.E.W.s have been used to improve Champagnes in the past, with the result that today the Champagne excels on all points. The main difficulty with this breed is to produce a standard shade of color both on top and bottom. If the belly color tends to be much lighter than the top color, use some darker Champagnes until this is rectified. If the P.E. White outcross has been overused, there is a tendency for the nose and set-on to be much paler than the rest of the body. This is a serious fault and, if possible, should not be tolerated in the mousery. Certainly never mate two mice with this fault together or it will become inbred into your stud.

If after repeated Champagne to Champagne matings the litters become too dark, introduce a Self Silver outcross. This will soon restore the lost pink tinge to the Champagne and may be necessary every fourth generation. Watch out for light extremities in this cross, however.

THE SILVER

"This is a delicate shade, as near as possible to an old silver coin [not the present cupro-nickel]. It should be sufficiently solid to leave no doubt of it being a Self. Eye Pink or Black"

The Self Silver is almost as popular as the Champagne, although it is a little more difficult to consistently produce winners from the former variety. This lack of success can perhaps be explained by the fact that there are so many shades of silver from off-white to light dove, and many people consequently set the "ideal" color differently. Whereas the Champagne is a P.E. Chocolate, the Silver can be described as a P.E. Blue. Like the Blue, the Silver carries a factor which causes a clumping or ticked appearance that can spoil an otherwise good exhibit, hence the special reference in the standard to the need for solidarity of color.

Mice in Maxey cages waiting for their turn to be judged.

National Mouse Club judge E.N. Smith is judging a Self Red while his steward watches attentively.

A peculiar feature of the Silver is a bleaching modifier which effectively removes pigment, to a greater or lesser degree, from the extremities of each hair. Each hair contains more pigment at the base, but this should only be evident when the coat is blown back and a bluish undercolor is seen. It could be argued that the Silver is not, strictly speaking, a Self. However, the bluish undercolor gives life and depth to the delicate silver color, without which it would be most unattractive.

As with all delicate shades, the breeder must balance his matings to produce the ideal color, taking care to guard against light noses and tail set-ons. The Self Silver is generally regarded as the best outcross for the P.E. White, since P.E. Whites so bred can be very useful for improving other varieties and also make good fosters. Apart from these specially bred Whites there is no other variety that can help improve the color of the Self Silver. Never use P.E. Whites bred out of Champagnes as they will ruin the ice-blue effect of the Silvers and instead give them a rusty tinge. It would take at least three generations before this defect could be bred out so that the proper silver color could be restored. Although the standard allows for pink and black eyes, Black-eyed Silvers are never seen, and I would question that they are genetically possible.

THE DOVES
"The color should be soft dove grey. Eye Pink"

The Dove was the last of the Selfs to be standardized and it is certainly the most neglected today. The majority of the ones that are now exhibited have probably been bred out of Silvers purely by chance. Originally the Dove was introduced to the fancy by the late Dr. W. Mackintosh Kerr in the early 1900's by crossing Blacks with Champagnes and then mating the resultant black litters together. Thus, the Dove is the genetic equivalent of the P.E. Black. Before 1966 an essential feature of the Dove was that it should have not a pink, but a ruby eye and the N.M.C. Standard stated, "The color should be soft dove gray, no darker than is necessary to retain the ruby eye." There was once some controversy in the fancy regarding eye color so the standard was altered to encompass any shade of pink, red or ruby. The color most affected by this was the Dove in both Self and Tan, for this is the only color which had to have a ruby eye.

I am relating this history because I feel that there is a definite correlation between the ruby eye and the correct top color, and perhaps breeders should aim for this

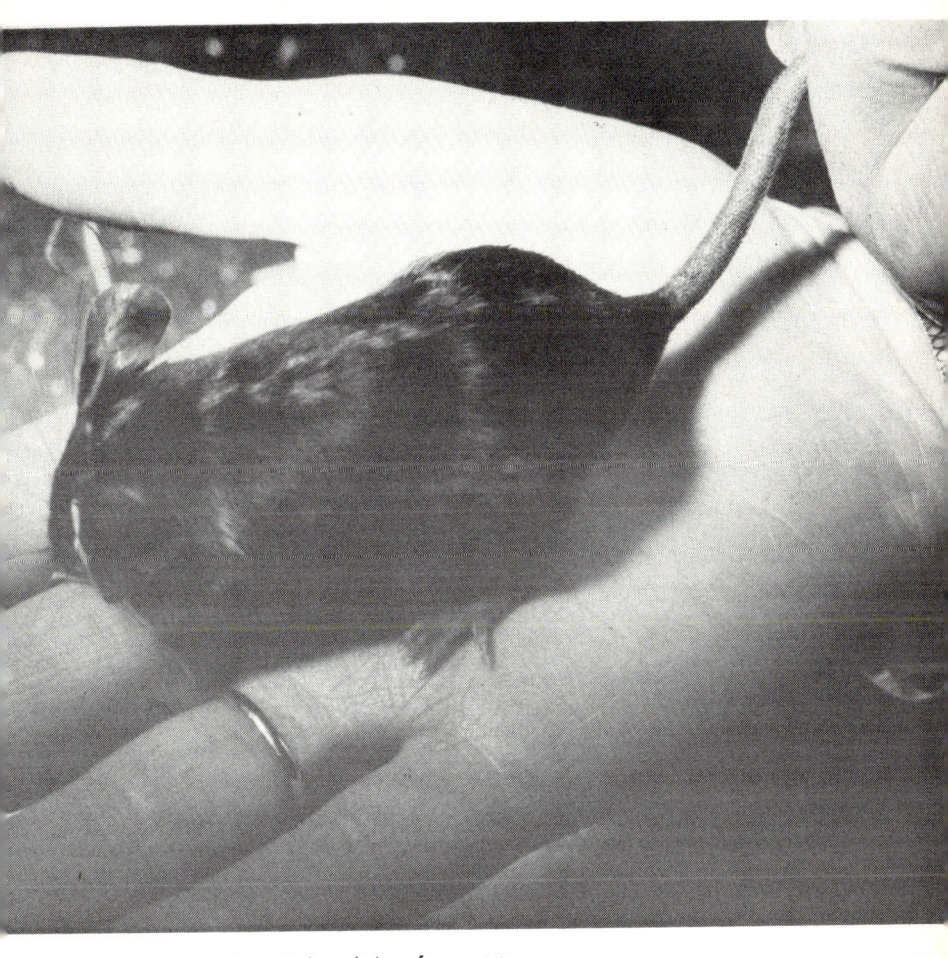

A new experimental variety of mouse.

ideal combination in an effort to popularize the neglected Dove. It is really a lovely and distinctive shade, and since it is genetically akin to the Silver, an excellent outcross for improving size and type is readily available. Take care not to produce Doves with light noses and set-ons in this cross. If starting a strain of Doves, I would suggest mating Champagne with Silver rather than with Black, because better type would result and Doves should appear in the first litters.

THE RED
"The color should be rich and deep, sparkling with no sootiness. Eye Black"

A good Self Red is undoubtedly a beautiful mouse, but it is definitely not a variety for the novice. The difficulties in breeding winning Reds are many, but the rewards are high when a good specimen is shown, and because it is such a striking color it will always have its followers. Yet mice in the Red group suffer from obesity. I do not profess to be an expert on genetics so I can offer no explanation for this, except to say that it is a fact of life for the Red. Continual breeding of Red and Red will produce small, fat, poor type specimens with dwarf ears and short tails.

To counteract these difficulties, an outcross is obviously called for. It has been found over the years that the best mice for this purpose are the Golden Agouti and the Cinnamon; indeed, many specialize in the three

A Sable mouse. The shadings on the flanks of this mouse make it a poor type.

Two views of a Fawn Satin mouse on its Maxey cage. Fawn is a beautiful color when satinized. Notice, however, that the animal shown is not an ideal type; it is too fat.

varieties with good results. Most breeders of Reds maintain that the Cinnamon cross gives the best results; due to the black factor in the Agouti pattern coat, the Red to Agouti cross tends to produce Reds that are rather sooty in color. The Cinnamon has no black in its make-up, however, and gives the best results possible. Red crossed to Cinnamon would give approximately equal numbers of each in the litters and it is then up to the breeder as to how his strain progresses. Possibly an even better outcross would be to the Cinnamon Tan, for the tan factor would also help the belly color of the Reds. If Cinnamon Tans are not readily available, they can easily be produced by crossing Chocolate Tan to normal Cinnamons.

"Hide-and-seek" is a mouse's favorite game. Mice feel secure in any type of tightly enclosed space.

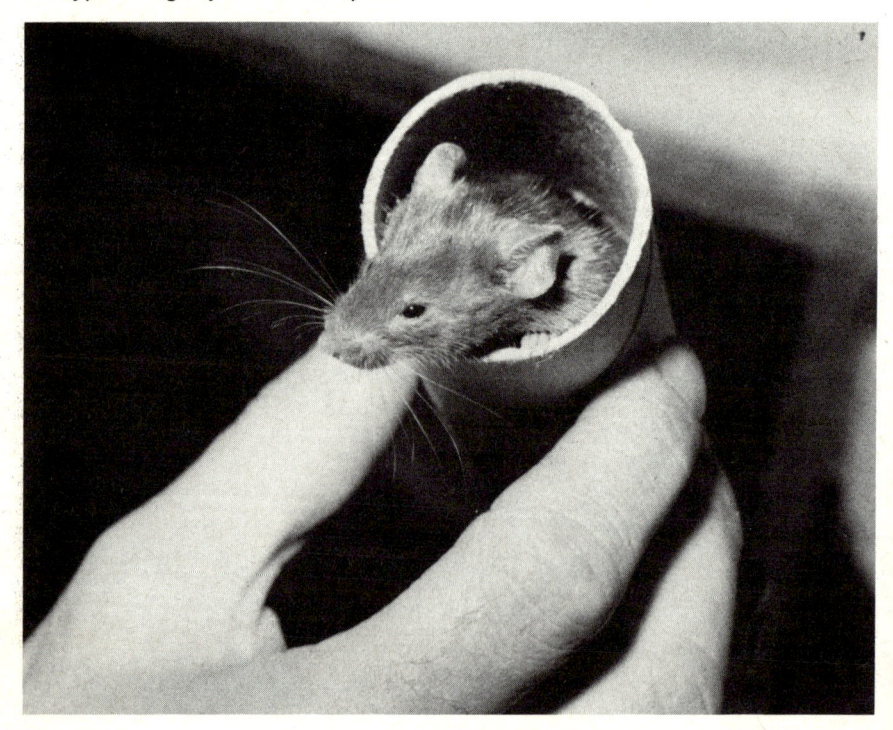

An entrant anxiously waiting for the great moment: is his mouse a winner or not?

Reds should be fed with special care; since they tend to put on extra weight rather easily, be sure not to overfeed them. Besides feeding the Reds bread and sunflower seeds, it may be wise to give them moisture: use water bottles or feed greens. If Reds do get fat it is likely that they will not breed. There is a case for breeding Red does from an early age, say ten weeks, and never letting them rest between litters, otherwise they could tend to obesity. Foster mothers have a part to play

123

here. It is not an exaggeration to say that Red breeding is a difficult task and is best left to the specialists.

THE FAWN
"The color can best be described as the deepest tan as on a Black-Tan. Eye Pink"

The word fawn is rather a misnomer, for the color of this Self is a strikingly deep orange, which makes it one of the most attractive varieties of fancy mouse. The Fawn is the pink-eyed equivalent of the Red, and if the Red could be described in terms of a color approaching that of an Irish Setter, then the Fawn is somewhat akin to that of a golden Cocker Spaniel.

A Self Champagne of good type and large ears. This individual was bred by the author.

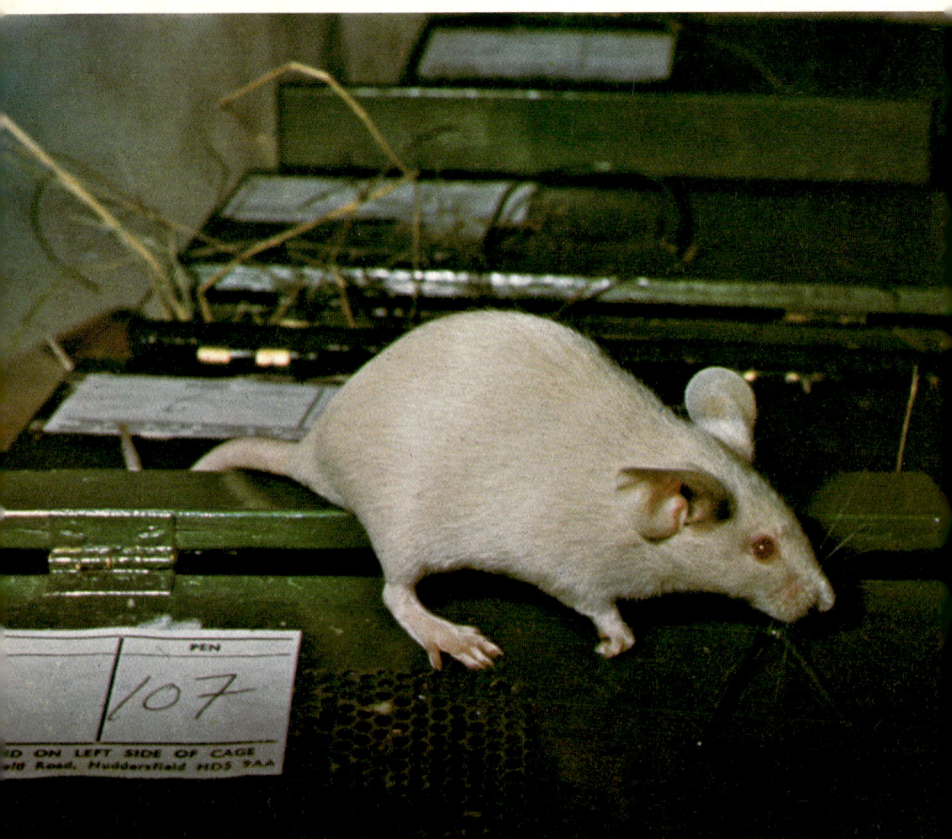

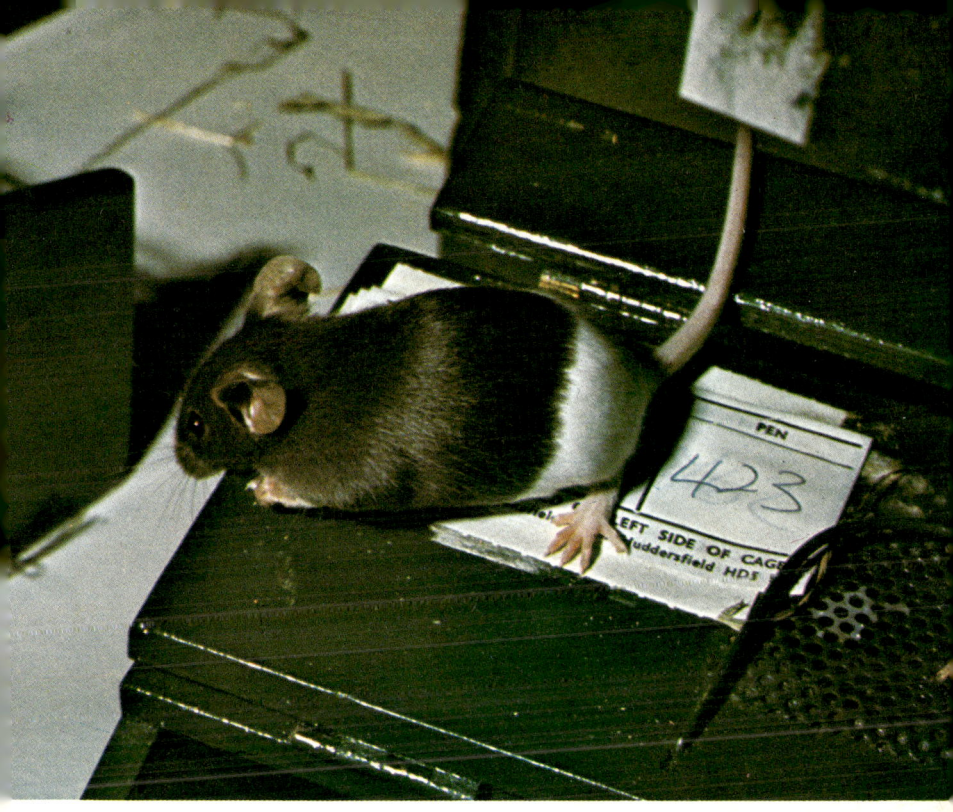

One of the marked mice category, a Chocolate White Rump.

Although the Fawn is closely related to the Red, the pink-eyed dilution factor renders the problems of the yellow group to a minimum. Fawns can be recommended to the novice fancier, although he may still encounter difficulties.

There is no reason why Fawns should not be of outstanding size and type, for there is a fine natural outcross to use in the Champagne Tan. This cross will undoubtedly improve all the points that the Fawn usually fails on, such as size, type, narrow skulls and small ears, and has the special advantage of helping the belly color. However, it should not be undertaken too often or top color will suffer, becoming too pale especially behind the ears and on the ears themselves. The best type of

125

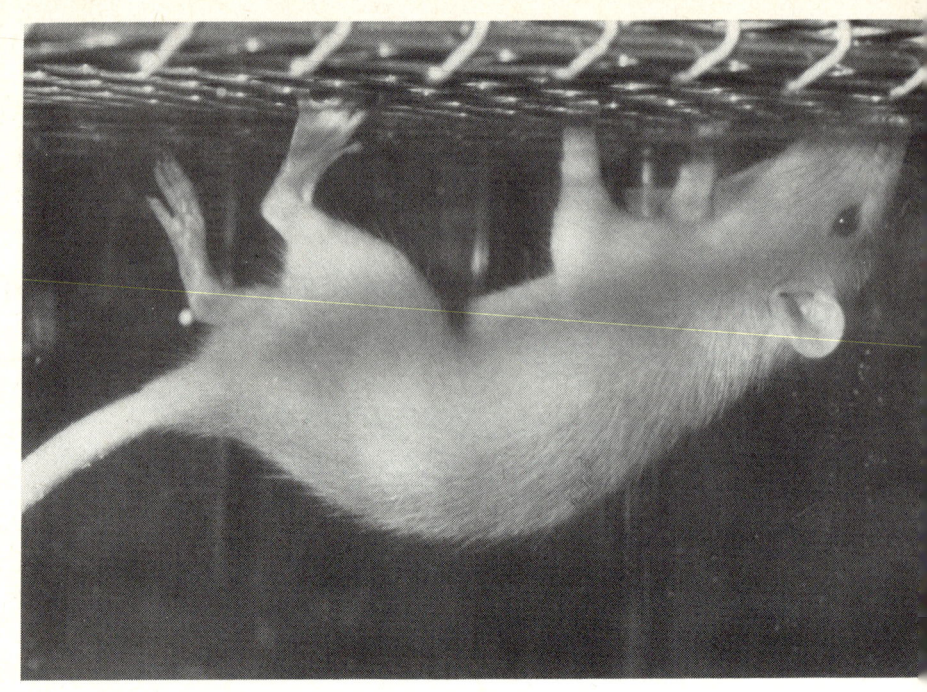

Agility is normally a sign of good health, but frantic nervous movements may be possible indications of some ailment.

Champagne Tan to use would be one that is not of the best color, for example one that is too dark and has the tan spreading on the feet, the tail root, behind the ears and up the jowls; in other words, use a Tan.

Any Tans bred from such a cross should not be reintroduced to the pure tan strain, for they will spoil the required delicate top color of the Champagne. They will, however, be useful for further breeding with Fawns. Both varieties can be kept with success, provided they are kept separately. Once size and type are established in the strain of Fawns, straight Fawn to Fawn breeding can be undertaken until such time as any failing is observed.

17: Tans

The Tan section as a whole is most popular and all the various varieties of Tans can be recommended to the newcomer. When the Tan was first produced in the 1920's, it was a product of Sables, and it can be imagined how poor they were at that time. The Tan of today is much improved and is never far away from the highest honors.

The N.M.C. Standard states: "Tans are recognized in any standard color, and the top color shall be laid down for these varieties. The tan belly shall be of a rich golden hue, as rich as possible, and there should be a clear line of demarcation between top color and tan, running in a straight line along the flanks, chest and on the jaws. There should be no brindling or guard hairs. eye color shall be as in the non-tan varieties. Color of feet should be—inside tan and remainder of foot same as top color."

FAULT

"All tan feet to be considered a greater fault than feet all same color at top color."

POINTS FOR THE TAN VARIETIES

Top Color	20
Tan	20
Feet	10
Condition—not fat, short and glossy coat	15
Shape and carriage	10
Size	5
Ears—shape, size and position	5
Eyes—large, bold and prominent	5
Muzzle—long, strength carried out to end	5
Tail—long and uniform, no kinks	5
	100

Although Tans are recognized in any standardized top color it is not possible, for genetic reasons, to tan every color. For example, it is impossible to have a Red or a Fawn Tan because these two varieties already have tanned bellies.

The six most popular Tans seen at every show are Black, Blue, Chocolate, Champagne, Silver and Dove. From time to time we also see Agouti, Cinnamon, Silver Gray and Pearl Tans.

It is fairly easy to maintain top color in Tans along with a fiery depth of tan color. The problem of Tan breeding is to maintain a rich tan without letting it spread to places where it is not required. A mouse would be severely penalized if it had tan around the tail root, up the jowls and behind the ears, for instance, but the most difficult fault to eradicate is tan feet. The standard

A Seal Point Siamese mouse. Note the dark nose and ruby eye color.

Commercial breeders are now able to produce mice that are uniform in size, color, life expectancy, resistance to disease, and even behavior. Photo by Dr. H.R. Axelrod.

clearly emphasizes what is required when it states that a mouse with tan feet is more at fault than one with feet all the same color as the top color.

The ideal Tan would be one that could be mistaken for a Self when viewed from directly above, and only when held aloft it betrays its true identity. The best way to improve feet is by selection. Keep some of those mice that, if exhibited, would be sent off as failing Tans, for these will have better foot color. If you persist in mating the richest Tan to the richest Tan, the color will spread to such a great extent that it will be difficult to keep it under control.

A more drastic method would be to mate a Tan to a Self of the equivalent top color. This will certainly help to improve top color and feet, but it would take at least four generations to re-establish the strength of the tan, by which time the same faults will be as evident as before. This cross can be employed, but is best left to the experienced fancier. The Selfs resulting from such a cross should *never* be mated back into a strain of Selfs, for obvious reasons.

BLACK TANS

The Black Tan is one of the most popular of all varieties, apparently because of the striking contrast between its jet black top color and rich fiery belly. It is certainly a variety much favored by newcomers as well as by established fanciers.

Black Tan to Black Tan would seem to be the most desirable mating, if only the best are selected at all times. Some fanciers use a Blue Tan outcross occasionally to improve size and type, for like the Self Black, the Black Tan is normally rather weak in bone structure in comparison to other Tans. So the breeder of Black Tans must watch his stock carefully, making sure that they maintain strength and vigor.

Of all the Tans, the Black Tan should theoretically have the strongest depth of belly color, so any failing Tan will not advance far on the show bench. Top color presents little difficulty, although odd white hairs should be watched for. Black-Eyed Tan varieties often develop tan guard hairs along their flanks, a fault which once established is difficult to breed out.

Another fault that the B.E. Tans suffer from is throat spots, which are small spots of the same color as the top color under the throat of the mouse. Obviously a black or a chocolate throat spot would stand out more than say, a silver or a champagne spot. Nevertheless, this is a fault that is prevalent in Black Tans and must be bred out. Careful selection of breeding stock is the answer; remember that all mice have faults but we have an ideal to aim for.

As stated earlier, never continually mate the strongest Tan to the strongest Tan or foot color will suffer. Bear these points in mind and your Black Tans will always be at the top.

CHOCOLATE TANS

The problems encountered in breeding Black Tans are basically the same for Chocolate Tans. Top color in Chocolate Tans is the same as in the Self Chocolate and should not be allowed to tend toward milkiness; a deep, plain chocolate is required.

Black Tan (not Blue breed) is the ideal outcross for improving both top and belly color if necessary. Beginners in this variety should be advised to purchase the best possible, mate like to like, and winners should hopefully turn up in every litter. Chocolate Tans have many admirers, so the novice should have little difficulty in obtaining good foundation stock.

BLUE TANS

The Blue Tan is the most controversial of all the tanned varieties; fanciers either love them or hate them. The problem with the Blue is that its belly color is nowhere near the same as that of other Tans. The reason for this is that the blue dilution factor has a reducing effect on the belly color as well as on the top color, which transforms the rich fiery belly of the Black Tan into a light buff color. The N.M.C. Standard states "as rich as possible," and with Blue Tans the richest tan possible is recognized by most judges; otherwise the variety would have no success and die out.

Just because special allowance has to be made for the belly color of the Blue, it does not follow that we should not be critical on other points. Top color should be a medium slate blue color and not a poor black as is often seen with mice of the strongest belly colors. Foot

131

Except for the absence of disease and deformities, other qualities such as uniform size, fancy coats, etc., are not that important for mice destined to be kept strictly as pets. Photo by Dr. H.R. Axelrod.

Having not developed any fur yet, newly-born mice appear pink; muscle and blood tissues show through the delicate skin. Hair starts developing immediately, but the eyes remain shut for 12 or 13 days.

color is generally better on blues than any other Tan, as it should be with mice of a weaker belly color. Size and type should be of a high standard.

The novice should have little difficulty in breeding good Blue Tans, provided he remembers that it is a dilute color and should be treated as such. Personally, I do not find the Blue Tan attractive, but I do feel it deserves a better deal on the show bench than it usually gets.

CHAMPAGNE TANS

The subtle combination of the delicate top color and a strong golden tan is very appealing and attracts many fanciers. Good coloring coupled with excellent size, type and minor points make the Champagne Tan one of the varieties that is never far away from the highest honors.

There are no serious problems in breeding this variety, although the breeder must be skilled to achieve the required pinky shade of top color with a good deep tan belly. Those Champagne Tans that have a good belly color are normally far too dark on top, a principal difficulty with all the Pink-Eyed Tans. Careful blending of shades will give the desired results, provided the breeder is patient. At all times thought must also be given to foot color and to tan around the tail root and behind the ears. This is certainly an attractive mouse and one that can be thoroughly recommended to the novice.

SILVER AND DOVE TANS

I have grouped these two varieties together as they are often bred in conjunction with each other; winners of both Silver and Dove have even occurred in the same litters.

The Dove potentially has the strongest tan of all the Pink-Eyed Tans and now that the ruby eye is no longer a necessity, it would seem to be the easier of these two varieties to breed to standard. While the top color may be perfected through continuous breeding of Silver Tan to Silver Tan, the tan would grow progressively weaker. Yet by using Dove Tans occasionally the strength of tan can be maintained. Conversely, the Silver can help the Dove by not allowing the top color of the latter to become too dark, or letting the tan spread to jowls, tail root, etc. The breeder employing this cross must be careful, however, or light noses will occur with alarming frequency. Both these varieties of Tan can be bred to good effect in one mousery, while the fancier has the added advantage of having two strings to one bow when exhibiting.

AGOUTI AND CINNAMON TANS

These combinations, although only occasionally seen, can be produced quite easily. Normal Golden

Agoutis and Cinnamons should be crossed to Black and Chocolate Tans, respectively, and the desired results should be evident in the first generation.

The tan should be very strong in these varieties, although top color will have to be improved after the first cross as it will be found to be too dark, for example, too much black or chocolate ticking.

SILVER GRAY AND PEARL TANS

These two varieties are rarely seen but are exceedingly pretty and deserve to be taken seriously. Perhaps the reason they are not popular is that it is difficult enough to breed normal Pearls and Silver Grays without the added problems of the Tan. If no foundation stock is available, the Silver Gray and Tan can be produced by mating normal Silver Gray to Black Tan. Fortunately, the black top will help the silver gray coloring, and by selection the tan belly will become deep and level after a couple of generations or so.

The case of the Pearl Tan is rather more complicated and is open to experimentation. I would suggest that the lightest top Silver Gray Tans be mated to normal Pearls. Henceforth the breeder must use his initiative in choosing his matings.

Size and type are failings in both these varieties and should not be overlooked in the breeding pen. A selected outcross would seem to be the answer and I would suggest Self Silver, although pied tails and light feet can be expected at first. Bear in mind that such experiments should be kept separate from normal breeding stock.

Certainly both the Pearl Tan and the Silver Gray Tan deserve more attention, although they are only for the patient breeder. If a good Silver Gray or Pearl Tan is exhibited it will undoubtedly be much admired by all.

An exercise wheel is a practical device that allows mice to get plenty of exercise in a confined area. Photo by Dr. H.R. Axelrod.

A mouse can get additional exercise by being handled. Hostility is also reduced as the mouse becomes familiar with its handler. Photo by Dr. H.R. Axelrod.

18: Marked

The marked section consists of only six varieties, namely, Dutch, Brokens, Evens, Variegateds, Rump Whites and Himalayans. Although it is numerically the smallest section, it is an amazingly popular one and classes for these piebald fancy mice are always well filled at all the shows.

Piebald mice, in particular Dutch and Brokens, seem to have a great attraction for beginners, especially young people. The great appeal lies not only in the undoubted beauty of a marked animal, but also in the novice's belief that it is easier to choose from his stock those animals with the most show potential, rather than to decide, for instance, between the different shades encountered in the Self colors.

While there may be some truth in this view, the beginner who is initially confused by the countless different varieties and colors can soon recognize the correct shades with only a little experience. I strongly advise the beginner against commencing with the marked varieties, not because they are harder to breed but because winners are few and far between. One can expect exhibition quality, if not actual winners, in every litter of Selfs, Tans, Satins and A.O.V. With marked mice, perhaps one in a thousand is a winner if you're lucky!

Nothing is more disheartening for a novice than lack of success. The disappointment in not breeding show specimens immediately leads either to changing to a different variety or giving up mice altogether. Breeding to a selected pattern requires an abundance of patience and perseverence besides a knowledge of how to balance matings in an effort to produce the ideal marked animal. It would be going against nature to breed to a selected pattern, and many difficulties would result. This applies equally well to English and Dutch rabbits, Tortoise and White and Dutch cavies, banded hamsters, Japanese hooded rats, pied budgerigars, etc.

When the seemingly impossible has been achieved, however, great credit is due to the breeder of the elusive "flyer." If such an exceptional marked specimen is produced, it is certainly worth more financially than any other variety. A good marked mouse will also last longer on the show bench, for whereas the show career of even a top class Self is normally finished by the age of nine months, a Dutch or a Broken could easily continue to win contests at the age of two years. It is for this reason that most of the N.M.C. Supreme Championships are gained by marked mice.

One other great advantage of the marked varieties is that by the age of three to four days any mismarked babies can be seen and destroyed. Culling this way with the other sections is a gamble, although consistent quality should be sought within the strain so that all the litter are reasonably good Selfs, Tans, etc.

The marked are not without their faults, however, since size, type and general stamina are generally not so good in the marked section. The reason for this is twofold. Firstly, the best marked are kept even though they may be runts of the litter. Secondly, extremely close inbreeding is required to retain all the good points of the strain as regards markings. The lesson is clear: No matter how good an animal is for markings, if it is weak and lacks stamina, do not be tempted to use it in breeding operations.

Above and Opposite:
In order to display the good points of a fancy mouse, it should be manageable. Well-behaved mice are not produced overnight; they are handled as early as possible. Trained mice will not jump or bite if held properly. Photos by Dr. Herbert R. Axelrod.

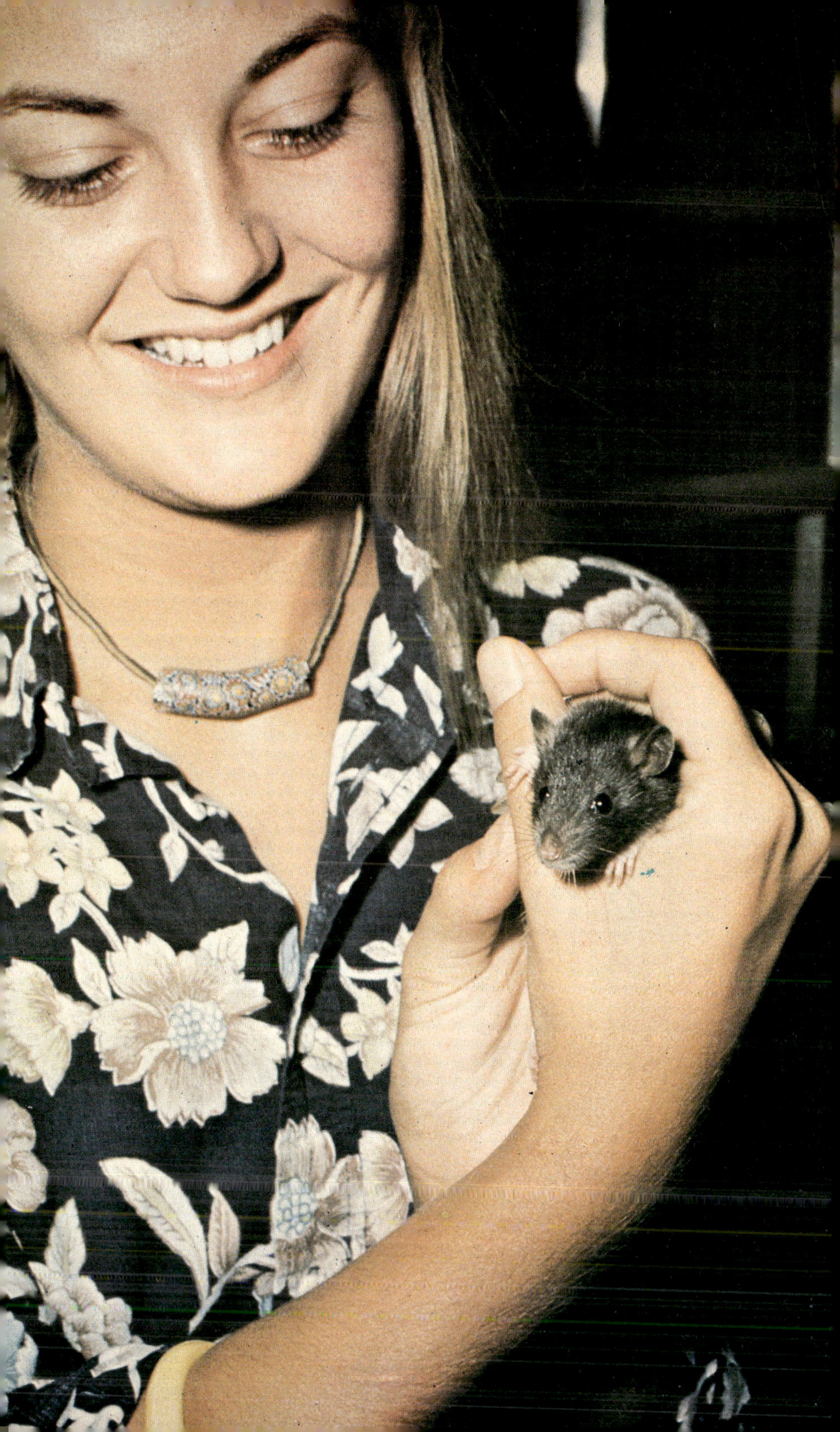

As fascinating as they might be, the marked mice are really for the experienced specialist breeder who can devote all his time and attention to breeding one variety and who is content to exhibit only occasionally. I suggest he also keep a second strain, say a good Self or Tan, so that he will have something to exhibit regularly and, hopefully, to win with.

DUTCH

The Dutch mouse is probably the most popular of the marked section, and indeed it has been one of the most popular of all the recognized varieties since the early days of the mouse fancy. Dutch markings are well

A Dutch-Marked mouse with balanced face markings that conform with the standards of this variety.

known to breeders of small livestock, for this attractive pattern is found in both rabbits and cavies. The present day Dutch mouse is far superior to the champions of yesteryear, which would now be termed wasters. Nevertheless, the mouse is nowhere near perfection as the rabbit, so improvement is always possible here.

The N.M.C. Standard states: "In Dutch marked, the face or cheek markings should be evenly balanced, a patch covering each side of the face, extending from underneath the eye but not to include the whiskers, and not to run further back than is necessary to include the ear, forming a wedge-shaped blaze from the nose tapering to a fine point between the ears. The cheek markings should not run underneath the jaw. The saddle should come well up from the tail to middle of the body and be clean cut top and bottom. The stops on hind feet should come half way between tip of toes and hock. The color of markings should be carried out in the ears. The colored markings may be any recognized color. Eye Pink or Black."

POINTS FOR DUTCH-MARKED

Cheek markings, blaze and color	20
Saddle—well up to middle of body	15
Undercut	15
Stops	5
Condition—not fat, short, sleek and glossy coat	10
Shape and carriage	10
Size	5
Ears—shape, size and position	5
Eyes—large, bold and prominent	5
Muzzle—long, strength carried out to end	5
Tail—long, uniform, no kinks	5
	100

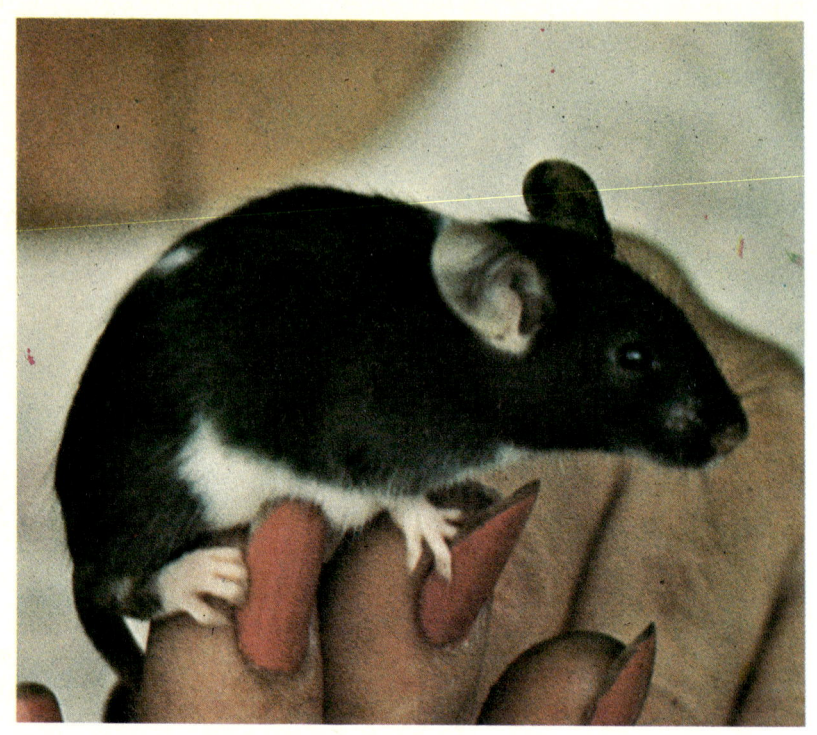

A sound mouse is easy to recognize. Good health can be judged from the general appearance of the coat, feet, eyes, ears, etc., and the behavior of a specimen under consideration. Photo by Dr. H.R. Axelrod.

The breeding of the perfect Dutch mouse is to a certain extent governed by Lady Luck. The breeder does play his part of course, and it has been found that the best way to be successful with this variety is to adopt a rigid plan of close inbreeding to fix the good points of the strain and breed out the imperfections. Because there are so many faults to eradicate, it may take several years to build up a consistently winning strain. Most top breeders adopt a line breeding system whereby son is mated to mother and daughter to sire for successive generations. This plan cannot be followed dogmatically of course, for it may be observed during operations that cousin to cousin would be a better mating in certain instances. Crossbreeding of two strains will never produce *consistent* winners, and the breeders therefore must stay within the family strain at all times.

The unfortunate outcome of such close inbreeding is that the Dutch is the smallest variety of fancy mouse and is somewhat stout or "cobby" in appearance. This factor is allowed for on the show bench, although weedy specimens, lacking in fitness and stamina, will not be tolerated.

By outcrossing to Selfs, type in Dutch can obviously be considerably improved. The first generation will be Selfs or Agoutis of a sort, but with pied tails and perhaps a white belly spot. When mated back to pure-bred Dutch the markings will improve with each generation, but by the time the ideal markings are obtained, the characteristically small and cobby Dutch will be evi-

A mouse is small enough to be carried in one's pocket and be shown to friends around the block. Remember, though, that not everyone enjoys having a mouse thrust at him. Don't use your mice for playing jokes; they're not toys. Photo by Dr. H.R. Axelrod.

dent again. Yet this cobby mouse does appeal to some because its elongated body would make its saddle appear to be slipping off the rear end.

Dutch does do not generally make the best of mothers because of their small size and low milk yield. It is a good idea to acquire another variety, say Whites or Champagnes, and use the does to foster some of the Dutch youngsters.

A good, high and straight saddle is certainly the most difficult point to fit in a stud of Dutch. Yet if the best marked specimens are mated together, then although the progeny may be well balanced, the saddle will become smaller and smaller.

It is easier to lose pigment than it is to retain it with any piebald animal, so keep the heavily marked does with high saddles, even if they are not of exhibition standard, and mate them to a good well-balanced buck that has a straight saddle and undercut and nice rounded cheeks. In this way pigment will be retained and saddles will not slip.

Some breeders practice breeding with mismarked does that have an odd spot or patch adjoining the front center of the saddle. This practice will give the desired result in time, although many mismarked youngsters will have to be culled. While the saddle may be improved, the undercut will suffer and the breeder can do little to remedy this except to select those mice with a high and straight saddle where possible. The real problem occurs when, after a decent saddle and undercut are obtained and the mouse has an abundance of pigment, the head markings are discovered to be too heavily marked. It is a case of one step forward, two steps backward.

The beauty of the cheek markings is lost if they are not symmetrical, and the color should not run back behind the ears into the collar or into the whisker bed and underneath the jaw. To counteract heavy cheek markings some breeders use mice with only one cheek spot. This method is worth experimenting with to lighten the head markings, although it should be attempted with caution. In his efforts to obtain perfect cheeks, the breeder must look out for the absence of color in the ears. This fault, known as flesh ear, will prevent any Dutch mouse from gaining top honors.

Since the breeder of Dutch has so many points to heed he can very easily overlook the tail and premature stops in selecting breeding pairs. The tail should be partly colored, so a pied tail is required. The stops, or white portions of the hind feet, should be evenly matched and straight all around. However, as the standard indicates, these two points are minor in comparison to the saddle, undercut and head markings.

Although the Dutch is recognized in any standardized color, the most commonly seen are Black, Blue, Chocolate, Agouti and Cinnamon. Occasionally Pink-Eyed Dutch are seen such as with Argentes, Champagnes and Fawns. The light color of the Pink-Eyed Dutch makes the stops difficult to see, if they are existent at all, and this is severely penalized by some judges.

In theory, color should be as good as the standardized varieties, but actually it will be found that even top class Dutch fail in color a little. Therefore, it is important not to overlook the quality of color in breeding stock, because even the best marked mouse will be held back if it is of poor color. For this reason it is probably safest to breed blacks, as the breeder will have a better chance of succeeding in this point.

Breeding Dutch is nothing short of an art, but even the most studious fancier has to be blessed with a large slice of luck to breed a Dutch that is difficult to fault. If the Dutch is for you, let us hope you are lucky enough to breed a "flyer."

Sustaining the mouse on the palm of your hand after having grasped the tail lessens the chances of its escaping. Photo by Dr. H.R. Axelrod.

A pregnant female especially should be handled properly to avoid possible injury to her and the unborn pups. Photo by R. Hanson.

BROKENS

Broken-Marked mice are nearly as popular as the Dutch, and it is certainly as difficult to produce a champion from them. There is no fixed pattern for breeding and no two Brokens are exactly alike. The ideal Broken would be a piebald mouse that has colored spots or patches placed with "regular irregularity" all over the body. The spots or patches should be of similar size, and there *must* be a nose spot.

The N.M.C. Standard states: "Broken-Marked. Eye pink or black. A Broken-Marked should be as far removed from an Even- or Dutch-Marked mouse as possible: that is to say, it should not have either Dutch cheeks, saddle, or any marking which may be considered evenly placed. The spots or patches should be well distributed all over the body and head, the more uniform the size the better, also the greater the number, and they should be free from brindling. There must be a spot or patch on one side of the nose."

POINTS FOR BROKEN-MARKED

Clearness, number, position and color of patches....45
Nose spot or patch (one side).....................10
Shape and carriage...............................10
Condition—not fat, short, sleek and glossy coat.....10
Size..5
Ears—shape, size and position.....................5
Eyes—large, bold and prominent...................5
Muzzle—long, strength carried out to end..........5
Tail—long and uniform, no kinks..................5
100

No definite statement is made in the Standard regarding the actual number of spots or patches, except to say that the more there are the better it is. The difficulty here is that when there is an abundance of spots or patches, the effect is one of overcrowding. The spots or patches then seem to run into each other, become joined together or appear evenly marked to some extent. The minimum number to aim at would perhaps be about eight spots, although twelve to sixteen, well placed, would be better.

The nose spot or patch is the only one mentioned in the standard and so it must be present. This important spot should be on one side of the nose only and may, or may not, include the eye of that side. Brokens with full nose spots and those without any markings at all are not desired and should not be used for breeding purposes. If the nose spot is on the right side, then ideally the left ear should be pigmented, and vice-versa. A separate eye spot can be an added beauty, although it is not essential. If it is supposed to be a separate spot, it should not run into either the nose or ear spots. The positioning of the remainder of the spots or patches on the body of the mouse are left to the selection of the breeder. For example, if a mouse was bare of spots down one side, it would be mated to a mouse that had spots on that side. In this way the matings would be balanced.

Even or symmetrical markings of any description should not be tolerated when breeding Brokens.

The standard for Broken-Marked requires the presence of a nose spot or a side patch. Many spots are desirable, provided they are well defined and are not touching each other.

Frontal view of a mouse with the incisors or cutting teeth exposed. All rodents possess two upper and two lower incisors. Photo by Ray Hanson.

Sometimes both ears are colored, but this is only allowed on the show bench if the color of one inclines towards the front and the other towards the rear. It is somewhat dangerous to use such a mouse for breeding purposes, as even ears may be the result. Even shoulder spots are one of the worst faults of Brokens, and mice with this fault should be discarded or the spots will continually reoccur. The body spots of the Broken should convey a feeling of irregularity, being placed in an uneven but pleasing pattern. They should not be evenly opposite each other or placed in a line or chain down the spine or down the sides.

When held by the tail a mouse will extend the body forward in an attempt to escape. This is a better position for observation than a hunched-up position. Photo by Ray Hanson.

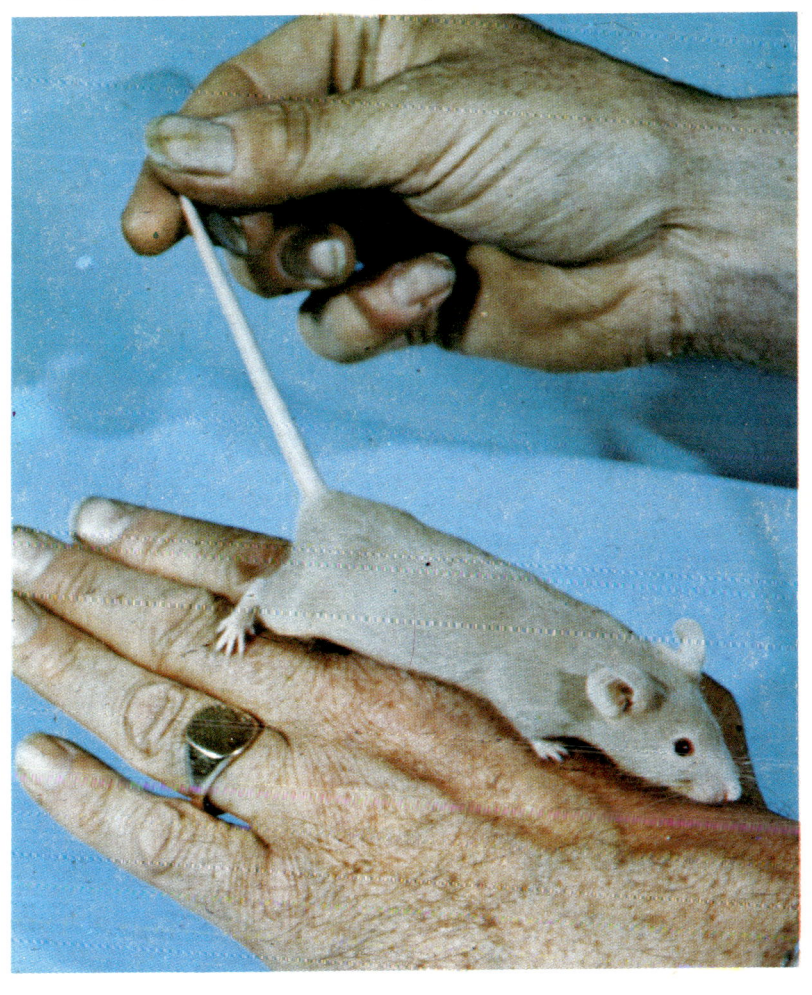

Any suspicion of a Dutch saddle is undesirable. Ideally the saddle should be split so that there is not one centrally placed spot, but rather spots on either side of the tail root, such as one on one side and two on the opposite side.

Color is very important. The standard requires spots or patches of clear color, having a neat, clean-cut appearance. They must also be sharply defined, not feathery edged, ragged in appearance or brindled. The Broken is recognized in any standardized color and, as in the Dutch, will be found in the popular colors, black being the most common. As with the Dutch, pigment can be easily lost by mating the best spotted mice together. To prevent this loss of color, the occasional use of some heavily marked specimens is necessary.

Type and size can be of a high standard. Brokens mated to P.E. Whites or Silvers will produce Selfs or Agoutis with white tails, feet and belly spots as described in the earlier chapter on Dutch. Only the does should be retained in the litters, and they should be mated back to Broken bucks. The next generation should produce heavily marked Brokens, possibly in various colors, and the does should again be mated back to their sires or uncles to produce Brokens of good size and type, of sound color and fit for exhibition.

If you do not possess unlimited patience do not attempt to breed Brokens. It can be a heart-breaking business. Many a youngster looks promising in the nest but as it grows, the patches join together or become brindled. Another near miss and all the breeder can do is sigh in exasperation.

EVENS

The Even Standard is one that is more open to individual interpretation than any other, by both breeders and judges alike. The Standard states: "Even Marked.

Eye pink or black. A mouse shall be considered even marked that is of recognized color and equally balanced in markings and free from runs. The more spots or patches the better, combined with pleasing effect."

POINTS FOR EVEN-MARKED

Clearness of markings, their position and color	55
Condition—not fat, short, sleek and glossy coat	10
Shape and carriage	10
Size	5
Ears—shape, size and position	5
Eyes—large, bold and prominent	5
Muzzle—long, strength carried out to end	5
Tail—long and uniform, no kinks	5
	100

Very few breeders specialize in Evens. In fact, most of the champion Evens of the past have been Brokens by chance! However, despite the latitude of the Standard, there is no reason why the breeder should not produce evenly marked mice to his own pattern. Any mice that would be discarded by the Broken breeder would be ideal to build up a strain. Thus for breeding Evens, choose those mice with a full nose spot, even ears, shoulder spots and a central spot at the tail root. This gives a basis of six spots or patches to work from, and with two or three more in the center of the body, would complete the ideal pattern.

One clue as to why the Even Standard is so sparsely worded is that in the early days of the fancy an Even-Marked mouse of the time would have been a poorly marked Dutch with one or two centrally placed patches separated from the saddle. This type of mouse often won best in show and championships, yet today it would be discarded!

Shredded newspaper serves as the nesting material for this gray mouse.

Opposite:
Wild mice subsist on any kind of food available. This mouse is feeding on a drift line along the beach where water-borne seeds, coconuts, sugar cane, etc. may be present.

Judges today require a mouse similar to the Broken in its shape and size of spots or patches, yet there is one vital difference: the Even Standard does not necessarily require spots or patches of similar size. The words "pleasing effect" are most important, for what is a pleasing pattern to one person may not be so to another. The Even mouse is one that deserves more attention and there is certainly room for new ideas here.

VARIEGATED

Variegateds were once popular and could be seen at every show, but unfortunately this is not the case today. Genetically, the Variegated is closely related to the B.E. White, and the decline of both these varieties has gone hand in hand.

The make-up of the Variegated is completely different from that of the Broken or Even. No solid patches are required, except "splashes" of color distributed evenly all over the body. The splashes or flecks of color should not be clean-cut, but rather ragged and brindled at the edges. The difficulty facing the breeder is to produce a mouse evenly distributed in color without solid patches appearing on the rump near the tail root or around each side of the head. When these solid patches are broken up, the body becomes too light in markings.

The standard asks for pigment underneath, but it is rare for the belly to exactly match the top, being either plain white or almost solid. Another fault that seems inherent in even the best strains of Variegateds is the frequent absence of pigment in the space between the ears.

A percentage of Selfs will turn up in the litters and the typiest of these should be retained and mated back to lightly marked Variegateds in an effort to produce the ideal. A good Variegated is extremely difficult to produce and it seems doubtful, considering the material available today, that they will ever be as good as they once were.

The N.M.C. Standard states: "Variegated. Eye Pink or Black. A variegated mouse shall be of any recognized color, evenly splashed over and under body, and must be free from any spots or solid patches such as are found in Evens and Brokens."

POINTS FOR VARIEGATEDS

Uniformity of variation and color	50
Condition—not fat, short, sleek and glossy coat	15
Shape and carriage	10
Size	5
Ears—shape, size and position	5
Eyes—large, bold and prominent	5
Muzzle—long, strength carried out to end	5
Tail—long and uniform, no kinks	5
	100

HIMALAYAN

The N.M.C. Standard describes the Himalayan mouse as follows: "Himalayan. Eye black or red. All markings to be as Himalayan Rabbit. Color or markings recognized in any color. Body color as white as possible."

POINTS FOR HIMALAYANS
Nose markings—well carried up to eyes............10
Feet markings—well up to hocks.................10
Ear markings—to include the whole ear...........10
Tail markings—to include tail root..............10
Purity of body color............................10
Condition......................................15
Shape and carriage.............................10
Size..5
Ears—shape, size and position...................5
Eye—large, bold and prominent...................5
Muzzle—long, strength carried out to end........5
Tail—long and uniform, no kinks.................5
Certificate 1970: E. Kitchen, Esq.   100

The Standard is self-explanatory, provided the reader has seen the very well-known rabbit of the same name: a white bodied animal with colored points to the nose, ears, tail and feet. However, although the mouse Standard reads any color of points or extremities, in actual fact the only known color is milk chocolate with pink eyes. There is no reason why, in time to come, other points will not be bred (possibly with black eyes), but at present the original color is the only one to have been popularized.

The Himalayan is of comparatively recent origin to the fancy and was produced by crossing Seal Point Siamese to P.E. Whites. This simple cross has made the

Mice and rats resemble each other greatly, but a normal mouse is always much smaller than a normal rat.

Himalayan comparable in all around shape and carriage to any mouse.

The main difficulty with this variety is to produce a mouse with dense points, yet having a pure white body color. The denser the points become, the less pure the body color becomes, especially around the rump area, which appears to be stained. This problem is also encountered in Himalayan rabbits and cavies. This defect is to some extent allowed for in the standard which says "as white as possible," but a mouse of impure color will be severely penalized.

Remember that the points are not expected to be a dark plain chocolate as in the standard for Selfs and Tans, but instead a light milk chocolate. The Himalayan gene is an unusual one in that it is temperature sensitive, and it is said that the points of the

A Self Champagne mouse. The standard for this breed requires pink eyes.

mouse become denser in cold conditions. However, do not keep Himalayan mice in such conditions, if for no other reason than the body color will suffer. Selection of the best all around mouse is the surest way to success.

Strictly speaking, the Himalayan is not genetically a marked animal, and many fanciers believe that it should be exhibited in the A.O.V. section alongside the Seal Point Siamese. However, the N.M.C. is not concerned with genetic classification, and for exhibition purposes the Himalayan is classified as a white animal with colored extremities. It has certainly provided a useful boost to the depleted numbers of the marked section and that is surely justification enough. If the points

a. Rump White

c. Seal Point Siamese

b. Himalayan

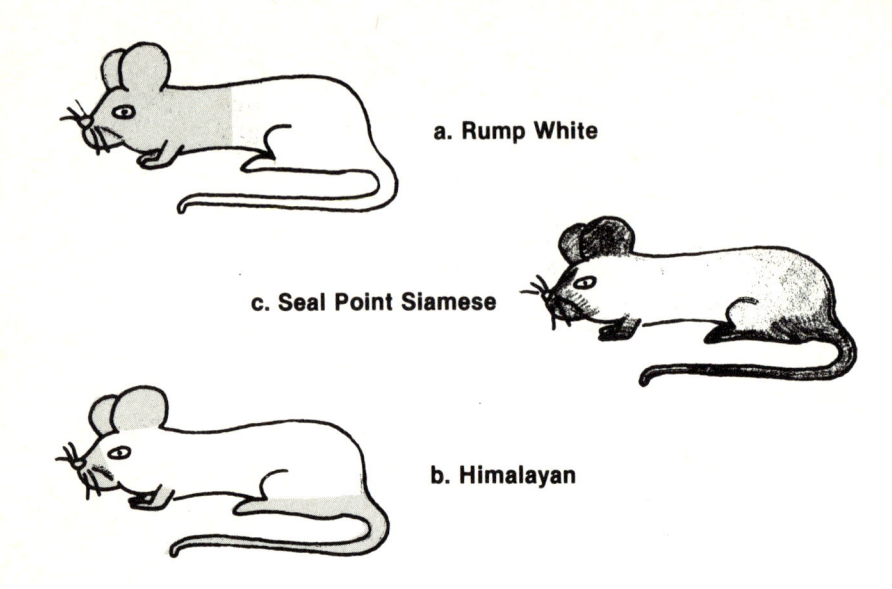

Some marked varieties of mice: (a) Rump White, (b) Himalayan and (c) Seal Point Siamese.

can be produced in other colors such as black, blue or red, the Himalayan could generate much excitement.

Unlike the other five varieties in the marked section, the Himalayan can be recommended to the beginner, for once a stud has been build up, winners can be consistently bred. The points do not begin to appear until the mouse is ten days old, and they become denser with age so do not discard any young mice believing them to be poor P.E. Whites.

RUMP WHITES

The Rump White has provided another useful addition to the marked section, and there is certainly no doubt that it is a piebald mouse. The original stock for this variety came from a laboratory and its introduction has provided a completely new gene, hitherto unknown to the fancy, as in the case of the Seal Point Siamese. The N.M.C. has formulated the Standard for the Rump

White as follows: "The Rump White is any standardized color having a white rump. The line of demarcation should be straight and encircle the body so that the lower third of the mouse, including the hind feet and tail, is completely white. The remaining color must be without any white markings at all and should conform with the standard laid down for that variety."

POINTS FOR RUMP WHITES

Color	10
Rump	10
Demarcation line	20
Feet	10
Condition	15
Shape and carriage	10
Size	5
Ears	5
Eyes	5
Muzzle	5
Tail	5
Certificate 1972: R. Meredith, Esq.	100

The original laboratory stock were not unnaturally lacking size, type, etc., but these points have been successfully improved by crossing to existing varieties. It has been found that the crossing of Rump White to say, Selfs, does not unduly affect the demarcation line since the Rump White area appears to be dominant to the Self. Rump Whites become apparent in the first cross, although they will probably not be of exhibition standard. The second generation is more likely to show improvement in size and type, together with a presentable demarcation line on both top and bottom.

The Rump White can easily be produced in any standardized color by the desired crossing. However, it is easier to obtain poorly colored specimens by indiscriminate matings than it is to achieve good sound color and so this factor must be borne in mind at all times.

White hairs in the colored portion and, more especially, colored areas in the white of the rump are two serious faults of this variety. Discard mice with any colored patches, flecks or odd hairs in the white portion (usually the vent area). It is exasperating to discover this or any odd loose colored spots on the rump, which could spoil an otherwise perfect mouse.

The demarcation line which separates the white lower third of the mouse from the colored portion is the

A Himalayan mouse. See the good bold eyes of this mouse.

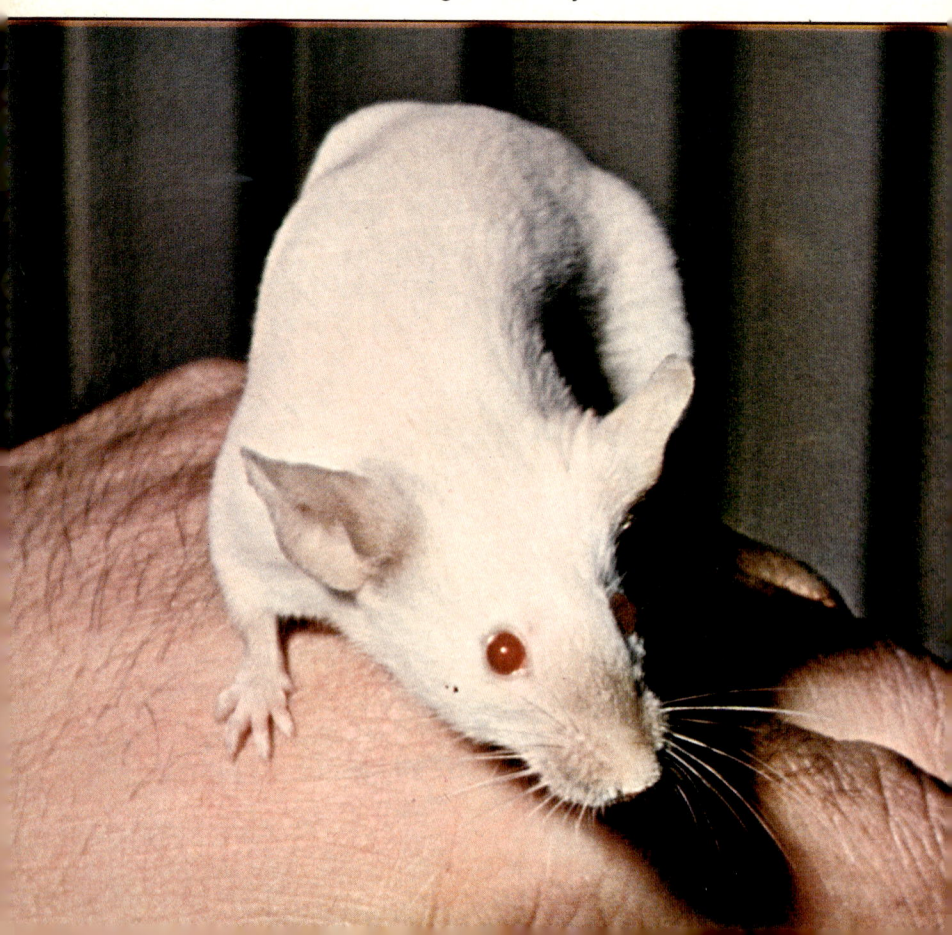

A Chinchilla mouse. Ideally, a Chinchilla should not have any trace of yellow or brown in its coat.

most important aspect of the Rump White. This line should be straight all around the body of the mouse without any runs, drags or brindling and should not be skewed in any way.

It is fairly easy for the top of the saddle line to pass the required standard, but the undercut is often sadly lacking: a zipper of white is prevalent in the form of a vee pointing towards the front legs. This unsightly defect will prevent many otherwise good Rump Whites from becoming best marked, and so must be given the breeder's full attention.

19: Any Other Variety

This section includes any standardized variety that cannot be classified in the previous sections and such mice are commonly called A.O.V. If a mouse has ticking, shadings or a coat mutation, it would not belong in either the Self, Tan or Marked sections but would be classified as an A.O.V. Numerically, the A.O.V. section is the strongest with some eighteen different varieties. Some of these breeds are very popular, some are of a very high standard and are capable of winning the premier awards, and some are neglected. A few are suitable for the novice breeder while others should be left to the experienced fancier. Above all else, the A.O.V. section offers more scope for genetic experiments than any other.

The ticked varieties are the Golden and Silver Agoutis, the Cinnamon, Chinchilla, Silver Gray, Brown, Fawn, Pearl, Argente and Argente Cream. The shaded varieties are Sables, Marten Sables and Seal Point Siamese. The Silver Fox (in black, blue and chocolate) is unique, especially the Astrex, Long Haired and Satins which are mutations of the coat. The Satin is not now classified as an A.O.V., and because of its immense popularity has been given a separate section of its own.

GOLDEN AGOUTIS AND CINNAMONS

These two varieties are very closely related, have a similar standard and are usually classified together at

A show is an excellent place to ask questions and add to your knowledge about mice.

N.M.C. shows in the A.O.V. section. As stated earlier in the chapter on Self Reds, these three varieties can be bred together to their mutual advantage.

The N.M.C. Standard states: "The Agouti shall be of a rich brown or golden hue with even dark or black ticking all through. The belly shall be golden brown, ticked as on top, and the feet shall match the body in color and ticking. Eye Black. The Cinnamon shall be of a rich golden tan, lustrous in color and level throughout top and under, with rich brown ticking clearly defined. No black ticking. Eye Black."

A Chinchilla mouse being examined closely.

POINTS FOR AGOUTIS AND CINNAMONS
Color	35
Evenness of ticking	15
Condition—not fat, short, sleek and glossy coat	15
Shape and Carriage	10
Size	5
Ears—shape, size and position	5
Eyes—large, bold and prominent	5
Muzzle—long, strength carried out to end	5
Tail—long and uniform, no kinks	5
	100

The Agouti coat pattern is that pattern and coloring that can be found in animals in the wild state such as rabbits, cavies, rats and mice. The coloring is fairly nondescript in this wild state, serving to camouflage the animal from its natural enemies. However, selective breeding by fanciers has greatly enriched the color, so that the Agouti coloring is very attractive.

A Blue Fox doe. In this photo the white belly and silver ticking as well as the teat marks are visible.

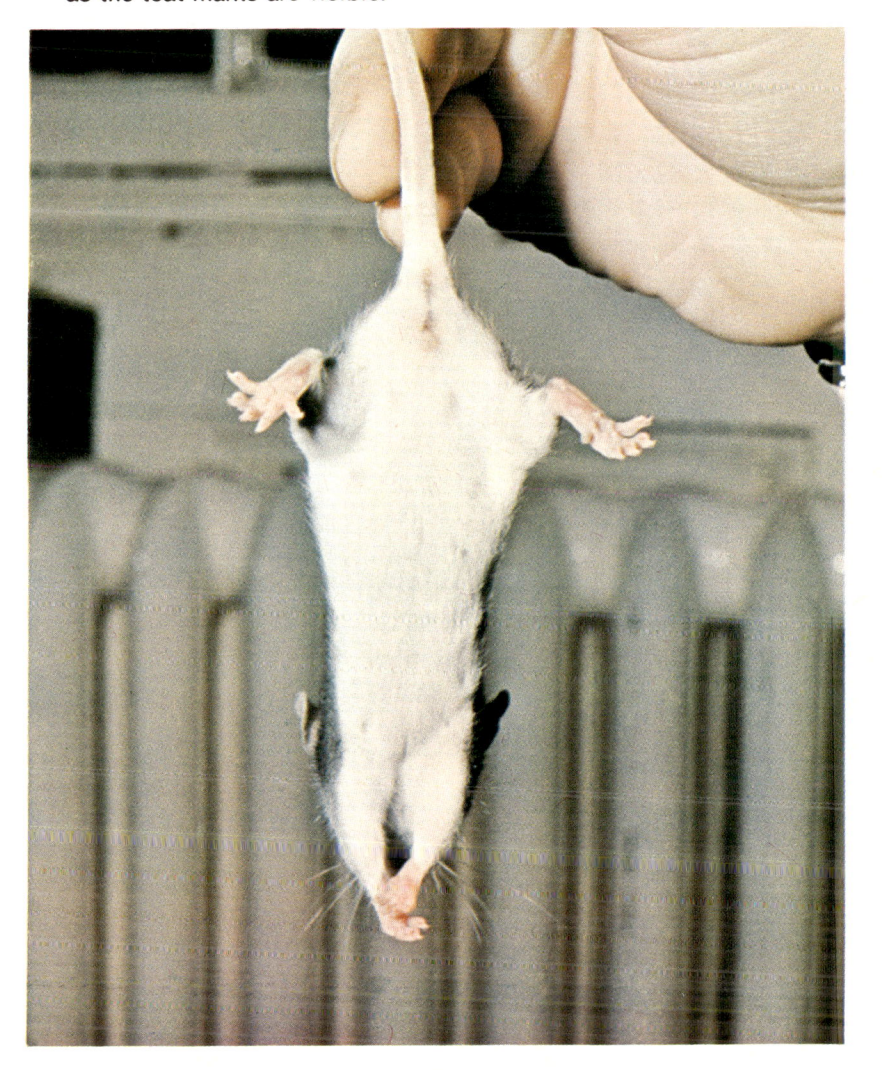

The coat of the Agouti consists of three colors: black, yellow and chocolate. Each hair at its base is black, followed by a bar of chocolate, and some hairs, but not all, are tipped with yellow. All the various color mutations known to the fancier are derived from these three basic colors. An essential point with regard to the Agouti is the "golden" effect which is determined by the amount of yellow pigment in the coat pattern. To improve this point the natural outcross would be Self Red. This cross would produce richly colored Agoutis, but type and minor points such as good ears and tail would be lost because the Red fails on these points. Therefore, this cross can be tried, but should not be used too often. A direct cross between Agoutis and Cinnamons usually produces poorly colored youngsters in the first generation, but if these crossbred youngsters are mated back to Agoutis, brighter colored mice should be seen.

If the Agouti is lacking in ticking, the Black Tan will correct this failing. Keep only does from this cross and mate back to an Agouti buck. Tans will continue to crop up and should be culled. It is easy to pick them out in the nest a few days after birth as the demarcation line along the flanks can be seen on those youngsters that are Tans. This cross can also improve size, type and minor points, provided Tans exhibiting these features are used. Yet it may take three or four generations of backcrossing before an improvement is seen and a winner produced. A fault that this cross can induce is tan around the vent area. This area seems to have a natural tendency to become tanned, so any Agoutis with an abundance of tan sould be discarded.

The Cinnamon is similar to the Agouti excepting that it has no black pigment. The absence of melanism makes the Cinnamon a naturally larger, typier mouse than its close relative, the Agouti. The Cinnamon has warmth of color, being a rich tan mouse with evenly defined chocolate ticking throughout the top and bottom. As with the Agoutis, the Self Red would improve background color, but loss of type and ticking would be the result. For Cinnamons, the Chocolate Tan should be used if the strain is lacking in ticking. Some breeders of this variety have used Fawns (Pink-Eyed Reds) to improve both type and color. This cross is worth experimenting with, and the word "experiment" should be stressed.

Belly color of both Agoutis and Cinnamons should match top color as closely as possible. The worst faults with both varieties are tan vents and poorly colored feet, sometimes with white toenails. Once a strain has been established mice with these faults should be discarded.

The word "rich" appears in both standards and is very important, for without depth of color these varieties lack fire and will not succeed on the show bench. A great advantage for breeders of Agoutis and Cinnamons is that they last longer for exhibition purposes than any other variety. Indeed, the correct color is not seen until about 12 weeks and improves with age.

SILVER AGOUTI

"Eye black. This variety is like the normal Agouti except that the golden brown pigment of the latter is replaced by silvery gray. Color: to be bright silvery gray evenly ticked with black. Undercolor: deep slate. Belly: to be silvery gray, as close as possible to the top but without prominent black tipping. Feet: to match top. Points as for Golden Agouti and Cinnamon." Certificate: 1969 B. Makin, Esq.

So reads the N.M.C. Standard, which is self-explanatory.

The Silver Agouti mouse is a recent addition to the ranks of the fancy and is an exact miniature of the cavy of the same name. Since the golden color is essential to the Golden Agouti, obviously the Silver Agouti must have a silver cast that is bright and clear and not bronzed in the slighest degree. This tendency of the cast to assume a bronze color is the most serious fault in this variety and can most easily be seen in the rump area.

This variety was produced after many years of patient work by crossing normal Golden Agoutis to Chinchillas, the resultant litters being mated together. Any youngsters with white bellies were discarded and those with the brightest silver tops were retained for further breeding. Type and size should be good in the Silver Agouti, although if a P.E. White outcross is resorted

A Chinchilla mouse. The belly must be pure white in this variety.

A Cinnamon mouse. Cinnamons and Agoutis are closely related; both varieties are ticked.

to, the genetic make-up should be black or its pink-eyed equivalent, Silver or Dove. Mice of the yellow group or any carrying tan would not be beneficial to this variety.

Unfortunately the Silver Agouti has not yet proven to be very popular and has not been widely accepted by fanciers or judges. One reason for this may be that it has to compete in difficult breed classes, often being matched against the superior Golden Agouti or Cinnamon. Another reason might be that fanciers who are attracted to the coat pattern and coloring of the Silver Agouti already have the Chinchilla to satisfy them. If the fancier is unable to obtain existing breeding stock, then the work must be undertaken with the raw materials of the best Golden Agouti and Chinchillas available.

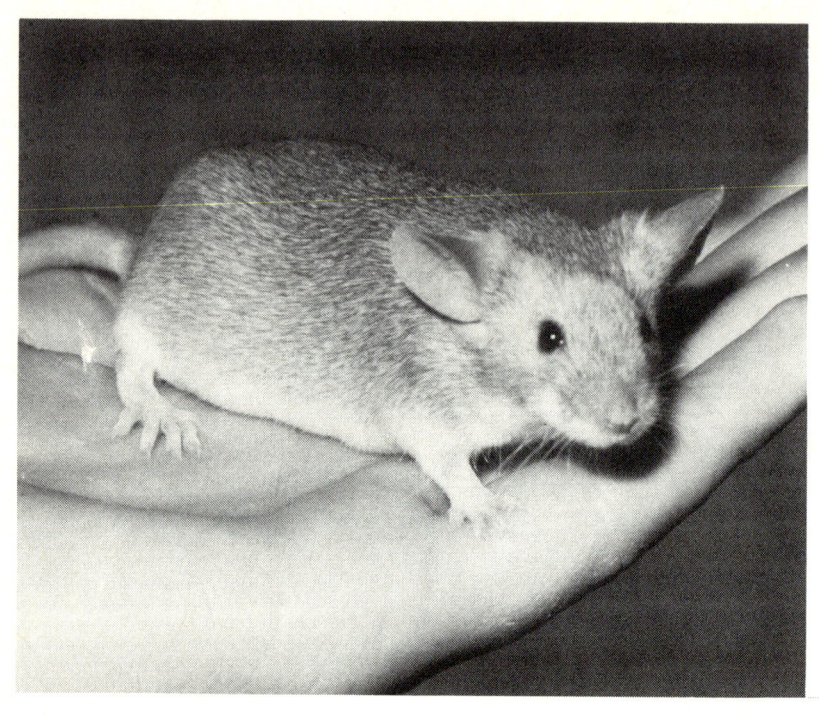

Many new breeds have been produced by crossing the Chinchilla with other varieties.

THE CHINCHILLA

The Chinchilla is, without doubt, one of the most important varieties in the history of fancy mice. The original stock came from a laboratory in the U.S.A. and were imported to England where fanciers improved them by judicious crossings to P.E. Whites. The following new breeds have been obtained by crossing Chinchilla to other varieties: the Silver Agouti, Silver Fox, Argente Cream, and Marten Sable. In addition, by crossing Chinchillas to Self Chocolates a new and improved cream color was produced. Some fanciers are also of the opinion that the Chinchilla had a part in producing Pearls out of Silver Grays, but this cannot be proven.

The N.M.C. Standard describes the Chinchilla mouse as follows: "Eye black. The mouse shall be as near as possible the color of a Chinchilla with slate blue undercolor and intermediate shade of pearl gray. Hairs to be evenly tipped with black. Color of feet on inside white, with remainder of foot the same color as body—as in the standard for Tans. Belly white."

POINTS FOR CHINCHILLAS

Color	20
Ticking	15
Belly	10
Feet	10
Condition—not fat, short, sleek and glossy coat	10
Shape and carriage	10
Size	5
Ears—shape, size and position	5
Eyes—large, bold and prominent	5
Muzzle—long, strength carried out to end	5
Tail—long and uniform, no kinks	5
	100

It can be seen from the standard that the Chinchilla mouse should be colored like the animal from whom it takes its name or like the Chinchilla rabbit. The coat is the same pattern as the Agouti but lacks yellow pigment in the hair tips. When mated to mice carrying yellow, the chinchilla factor dilutes this color to pale cream or white.

The most important points to bear in mind when exhibiting "Chins" (as they are commonly called) are the top color, belly color and freedom from molt. The top color should have a bluish cast which is lively and very attractive. However, many Chins have a brownish tinge which can more easily be seen by holding the mouse in one hand and brushing the coat with the other

A Self Red mouse. Small ears are a prevalent fault of this variety.

towards the rump. If the mouse has a brown cast this will soon be evident and such mice should not be used for breeding. It is probable that such a cast was caused by using P.E. Whites of the wrong color make-up, such as Chocolates or Champagnes. Black and Blue are the obvious choices, although Silver or Dove would give better type, size, etc. When using such a cross to a pink-eyed variety, pied tails will continually re-occur, but these mice should be culled from the nest. The belly should be pure white in color, well covered and not thinly furred. For this reason most Chins exhibited are bucks, being usually superior to does in this respect.

By far the worst problem with this variety is molt. No exhibition animal can succeed if its coat is molting and the Chinchilla seems to molt more than any other mouse. Why this is so is not clear, but it is certainly a nuisance for the exhibitor of the variety. Once the molt commences it never seems to finish on the show bench. Thus, a fairly large stud is necessary if the fancier wishes to exhibit regularly. Apart from the tendency to molt, the Chinchilla is a good variety for the newcomer and affords plenty of scope for those who like to experiment.

Foot color should also be mentioned. The original stock had all white feet and this fault has not yet been corrected. Good feet can be produced only at the expense of top and belly color, so judges allow for this factor.

A Dutch-Marked mouse crawling on the top of a Maxey show cage.

SILVER GRAY, FAWN OR BROWN

Here again we have varieties of mice that have their equivalent in the fancy rabbit. The silvered coat is one that has a basic ground color interspersed with different colored hairs. It should not be confused with the similarly named Silver Agouti, for it is completely different both in appearance and in genetic constitution. The Silver Gray is the most common of the three colors, the Brown and Fawn being virtually extinct.

The N.M.C. Standard states: "Eye black except for Silver Fawns which may be pink or black. The undercolor in Grays should be rich blue-black; in Fawns a deep bright orange; in Browns a rich deep chestnut. The silvering should be even throughout carried well onto feet. Silver Grays are recognized in three shades, namely, dark, medium and light."

POINTS FOR SILVER GRAYS, BROWNS AND FAWNS

Color	30
Ticking—sharp, bright and even throughout	20
Condition—not fat, short, sleek and glossy coat	15
Shape and carriage	10
Size	5
Ears—shape, size and position	5
Eyes—large, bold and prominent	5
Muzzle—long, strength carried out to end	5
Tail—long and uniform, no kinks	5
	100

The silvering factor in Silver Grays is the result of four types of hairs intermixed: (1) all black (2) all white (3) black with white tips and (4) black, gray and white banded. The silvered animal is genetically unique as it carries a gene for partial albinism, i.e., white hairs.

When in the nest, the babies appear to be Selfs, but by four to five weeks the silvering begins to come through and increases with age. The face, rump and feet are the last areas to finish silvering. Many otherwise good Silver Grays suffer from dark extremities in that the nose, tail root and feet are solid and have no ticking, a fault that is severely penalized. A ticked mouse must be exhibited perfectly free from molt or it will not appear to be level. The Silver Gray, like the Chins, suffers badly from being "stuck in the molt."

Although recognized in three shades, the darkest is considered to be the most desirable, provided the silvering is level. The rich blue-black undercolor can be achieved without any difficulty on the darker shades, but it is easier to maintain level ticking on the medium and light shades. Therefore, the breeder must blend the different shades together to capture both good points. The ideal required by most judges would be a black mouse with sharply defined ticking, with the black carried to the base of the hair.

The most logical outcross is Self Black. As silvering is recessive in Selfs, the first generation of such a cross would all be Blacks, but this situation could be improved by mating back to Silver Grays. A fault to watch for after this cross is tan hairs around the vent. This variety often fails in size, type and minor points, so any improvement made in these areas would be beneficial. Outcrosses to P.E. Whites or Silvers should be attempted, although the usual defects of pied tails and light feet would follow. The Silver Gray when shown to perfection can be very pretty indeed but is not an easy variety for the novice to start with.

There is no absolutely successful method of breeding these two varieties, and there is tremendous scope for experimentation. A good strain of Silver Grays would be initially required and should be crossed to Self

Chocolates, Cinnamons and Agoutis. After a couple of generations some brownish mice would be produced that show silvering. The best of these should be retained for further breeding and then can be crossed to Fawns and Reds. There are other methods but none has yet produced a mouse approaching the ideal.

An Agouti Dutch mouse. A truly straight saddle is not easy to produce in Dutch mice.

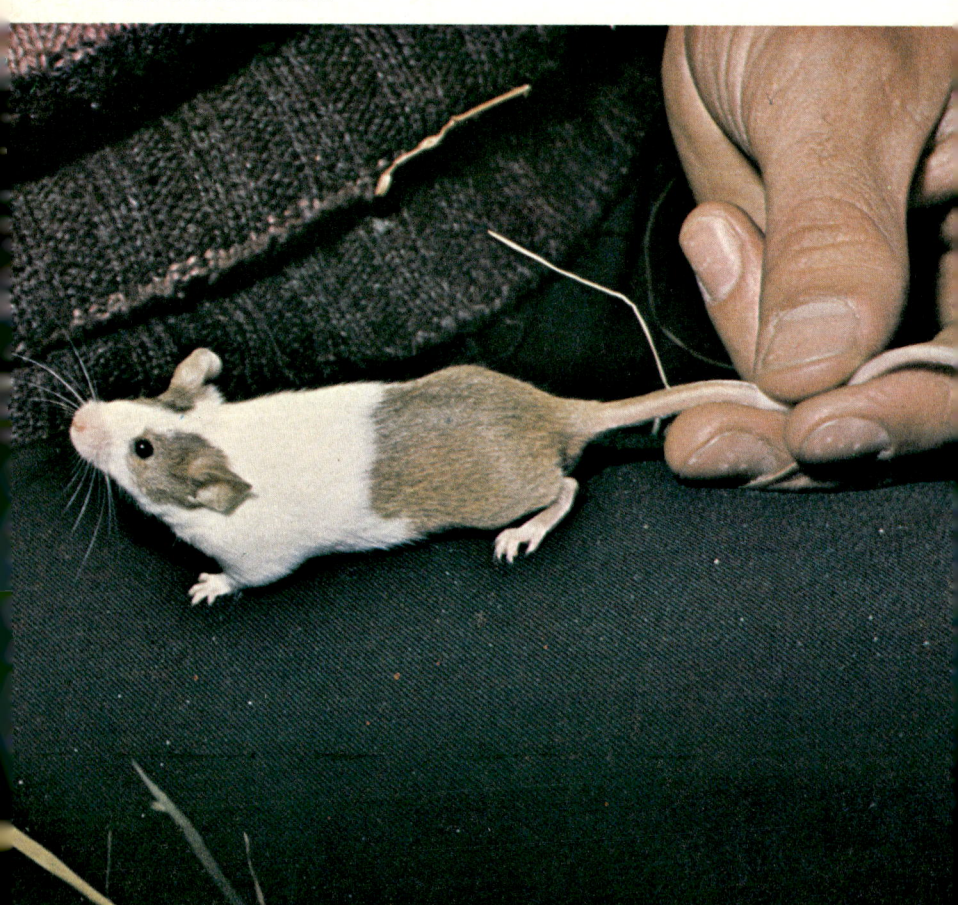

A Black Fox mouse. Some silver ticking can be seen along its flanks.

PEARLS

The Pearl mouse is very closely related to Silver Grays. No records are available to describe exactly how the Pearl was produced, yet it must carry a gene for silvering in its make-up.

The N.M.C. Standard is as follows: "Eye black. A Pearl mouse shall be of the palest silver, shading to whitish undercolor. Each hair shall be delicately tipped with gray or black and carried out top and belly. Points as for Silver Grays, Fawns, Browns. Certificate 1933: Mrs. E.D. Blowers.

If the fancier is unable to obtain ready-made Pearls, then it is possible to produce them from light Silver Grays which lack good undercolor. This may take some time, but by constantly mating the lightest together (provided they have a whitish undercolor), the Pearl will eventually be produced. Keep in mind that this variety is not known for outstanding size or type. One unusually excellent feature, however, is a large, bold, bright eye which many other varieties lack. Other varieties would benefit greatly if they had eyes such as those found in the Pearl.

The molt also badly affects the Pearl for exhibition purposes, but a good one shown in full coat is beautiful to say the least. It should be a delicate hue of silvery-gray shading to a whitish undercolor. Note that the standard says "whitish" not "white" undercolor. This whitish undercolor readily distinguishes the Pearl from the lightest Silver Gray. Each hair should be delicately tipped with pigment, for it is the evenness of tipping combined with the light undercolor that gives the final pearly appearance.

ARGENTES

The Argente is an extremely attractive variety and is never far away from the top awards. Genetically the

Argente is a Golden Agouti carrying the pink-eyed dilution factor. Although first produced in the 1930's, it never became popular and died out until about 1956 when some fanciers bred it purely by chance by mating P.E. Whites (Silver bred) to Agoutis. Since then the Argente has gone from strength to strength and has won as many red cards as any A.O.V.

The N.M.C. Standard states: "Eye pink. An Argente mouse shall be of a delicately blended shade of light fawn and silver, as the Self Silver, level throughout, and the two colors so evenly intermingled as to give the appearance of shot silk. The undercolor to be blue, as dark as possible in shade. The belly to be a golden fawn and as similar to the top as possible. Feet to match top."

POINTS FOR ARGENTES

Color	30
Evenness of blending	15
Undercolor	10
Condition—not fat, short, sleek and glossy coat	10
Shape and carriage	10
Size	5
Ears—shape, size and position	5
Eyes—large, bold and prominent	5
Muzzle—long, strength carried out to end	5
Tail—long and uniform, no kinks	5
Certificate 1935: L. Madeley Esq.	100

The essential feature of the Argente (a French word that means silver) is the beautiful shot silk appearance brought about by the intermingling of light fawn and silver. It must be remembered that the Argente carries the Agouti coat pattern and as the

A Blue Fox doe.

Agouti, its color deepens with age. This, however, is not necessarily an advantage to the Argente because the deeper fawn will tend to mask the silver hairs, and although the mouse will be level, it will lack the shot silk effect. Those Argentes that show too much silver are equally at fault because they appear to have silver spines with fawn only on the flanks. Adults with this defect should be discarded.

The darker Argentes might well win as youngsters but tend to be too dark as adults. Be sure that these mice retain a reasonable blue undercolor and sound belly color, since these two areas can become too pale. The undercolor, which can easily be seen by blowing into the mouse's coat, is a tricky feature because the paler the top color becomes, the paler the blue becomes. A dark blue is not required, the standard merely states "as dark as is possible." If the belly color becomes too pale, it is definitely time to use a darker mouse in the breeding pens; otherwise points will be lost on the show bench.

There are two different outcrosses for Argentes: either the P.E. Silver or Dove or the P.E. Fawn. The first one would produce better type Argentes, but the Fawn would perhaps give a more level color and would better improve belly color. Perhaps the answer would be to use Silver Tans. Whatever outcross is used it must be of the very highest quality for size, type, ears, tail,

A Silver Gray mouse. Uneven ticking is not desirable in this fancy mouse.

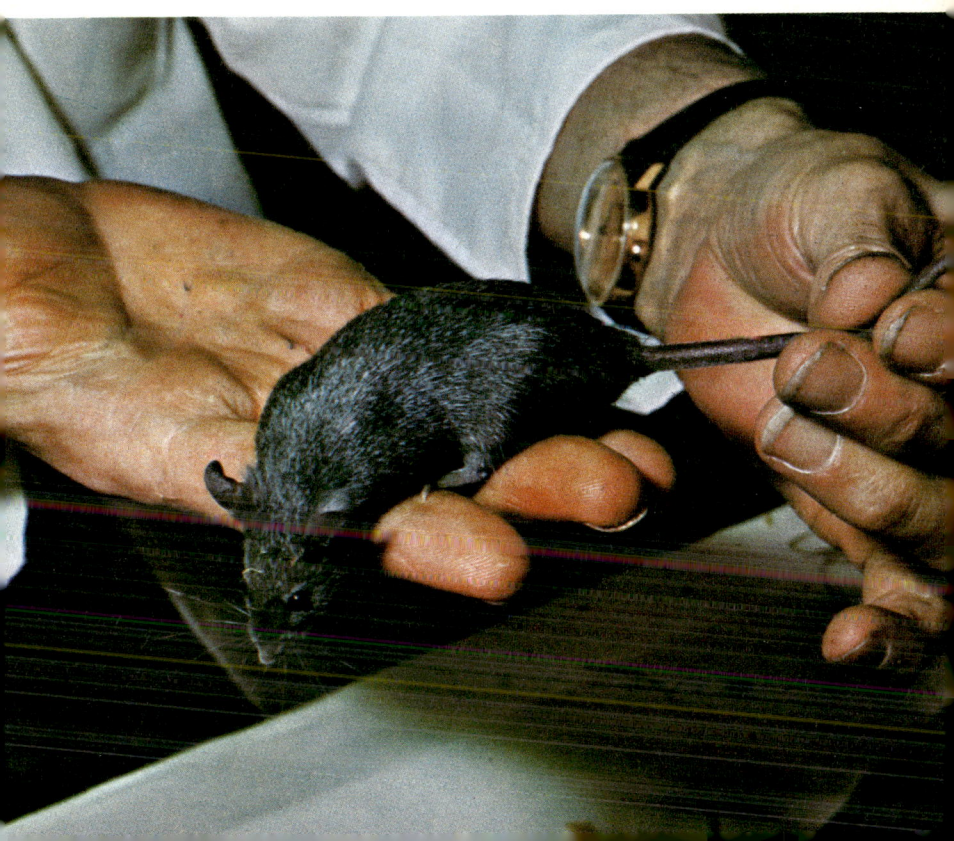

etc., because the Argente should excel in all these features.

THE ARGENTE CREME

If the Argente can be called a P.E. Agouti, then the Argente Creme can be called a P.E. Chinchilla. Another way of describing this mouse would be a Chinchillated Argente.

The N.M.C. Standard describes the Argente Creme thus: "Eye pink. An Argente Creme mouse shall be of a delicately blended shade of deep cream and silver. The undercolor to be an extremely pale blue. Feet the same color as body. Belly white."

POINTS FOR ARGENTE CREME
```
Color..............................................30
Undercolor.........................................15
Belly..............................................10
Condition—not fat, short, sleek and glossy coat.....10
Shape and carriage.................................10
Size................................................5
Ears—shape, size and position.......................5
Eyes—large, bold and prominent......................5
Muzzle—long, strength carried out to end............5
Tail—long and uniform, no kinks.....................5
                                                  100
```
Certificate 1967: B.J. Cooke, Esq.

The Argente Creme can be fairly easily produced by introducing the pink-eyed dilution factor to the Chinchilla through the normal Argente. The first generation will be Golden Agoutis, but these youngsters interbred will produce the Argente Creme. This variety is similar in appearance to the normal Argente except that the light fawn is replaced by deep cream. Because of the Chinchilla factor the golden fawn of the belly

One of the author's champion B.E. Creams with two of its prizes. Certificates are awarded to a mouse that wins 5, 10, 15, 20 or 25 first prizes (single, double, treble, quadruple and supreme champions, respectively).

(which is really tan) is reduced to pure white. It is essential that the top is *deep* cream to form a contrast to the belly color. The mixture of deep cream blended with silver should make the top color really sparkle when shown in tip-top condition. Like the normal Argente, the Argente Creme has a blue under color, but this should be "extremely pale" because this mouse is actually a diluted variety. Poor specimens are soon overlooked but a good one is very attractive, and although it is one of the newer varieties, the Argent Creme is now reasonably popular.

SABLES

The Sable is a distinctive mouse that is shaded rather than ticked and should resemble the popular rabbit of the same name. Once light, medium and dark shades were recognized, but now only the darkest is required which is good for the breed, since the lighter shades resemble poor Reds and are very unattractive.

The N.M.C. Standard describes the Sable in the following manner: "Eye black. The top color shall be a rich dark brown, as dark as possible, from nose to tail root; the belly color to be as rich a golden tan as possible, and the shading from top to belly to be gradual, even and pleasing, with no line of demarcation, nor any blotch, patch, ticking or streakiness. There should be no white hairs whatsoever."

A Black Fox mouse. Notice the great contrast between the pure white belly and black upper part of the body.

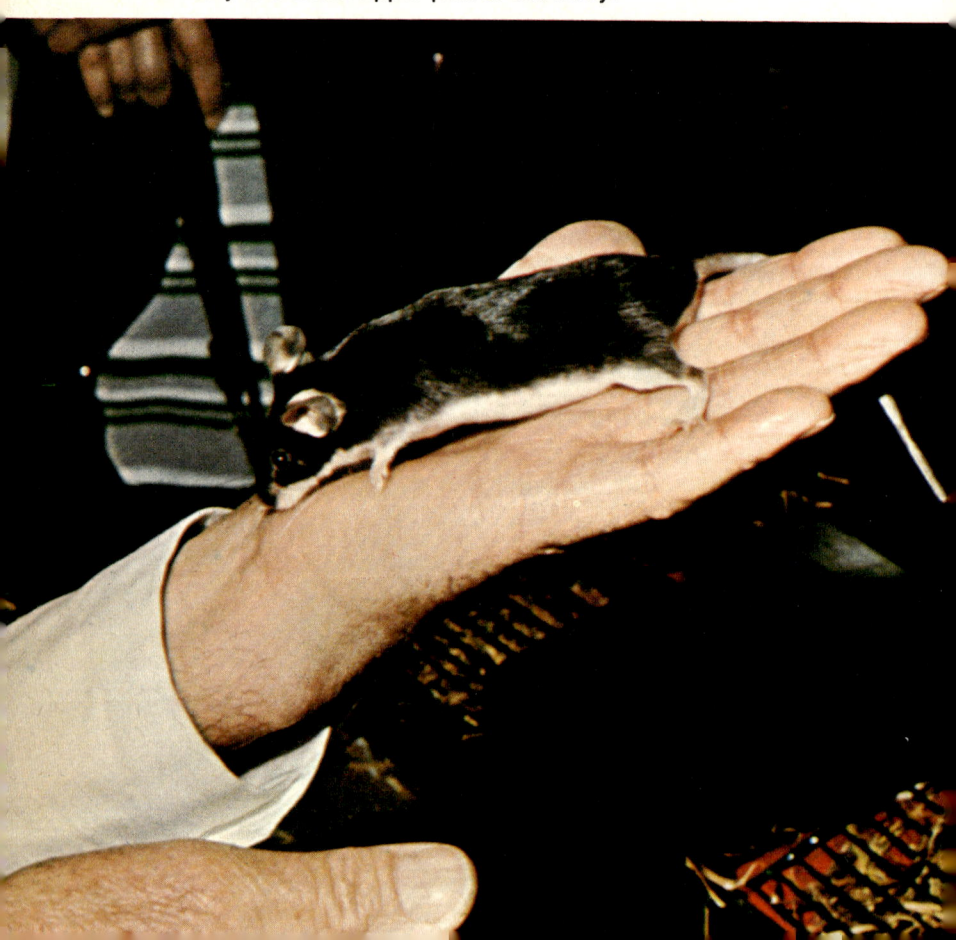

A nondescript type of mouse—but still a fit and healthy animal.

POINTS FOR SABLES
Color	35
Level shading	15
Condition—not fat, short, sleek and glossy coat	15
Shape and carriage	10
Size	5
Ears—shape, size and position	5
Eyes—bold, large and prominent	5
Muzzle—long, strength carried out to end	5
Tail long and uniform, no kinks	5
	100

Genetically, the Sable is a member of the yellow group and as such encounters all the difficulties of that group. Obesity is a problem, not only because it can lead to sterility, but also because of failing of type for exhibition purposes. The anemic lethal factor is also linked to the yellow gene, so that when two mice of this group are mated together, approximately 25% die before birth. Accordingly, Sable litters are usually small in number.

To overcome these difficulties a selected outcross is the only answer. It has been found that the Black Tan is the most suitable because not only does this variety help to keep the top dark and the belly fiery, but it also improves size, type and vigor. If no Sables are readily available, a strain can easily be derived by using Black Tans and Self Reds. The effect of this cross is that certain genes are transmitted to the Red which produce the dark brown coloration along the spine or dorsal region, from head to tail. Sables will arrive in the first generation and they can be improved in subsequent matings of Sable to Sable.

It is essential that the intermediate shadings from the dark top to the rich fiery tan belly be gradual. There should be no evidence of ticking or any demarcation line as in a Tan. A gradual blending from dark to light is what is required.

Black Tans and Agouti Tans will appear among the Sable litters. The Agouti Tans should be discarded as they will not be of benefit, but an occasional Black Tan can be retained to mate back into the Sables. Some breeders prefer to use a fresh Black Tan of outstanding type and color to maintain vigor in the Sable, and this outcross may be needed every third or fourth generation. If the Sables are becoming rather dark and lack the gradual shadings, a good Chocolate Tan outcross may help.

The Sable's worst failing on the show bench is its

A Sable showing the required dark coat.

notorious light nose. Even the best strains have a tendency to acquire this patch of red which intensifies with age. It seems to be an inherent fault in the Sable and occurs naturally on those specimens that are full of fire. Selection of breeding stock is the only way to try to eradicate this fault.

The Sable is one of the oldest varieties of fancy mouse but has never gained much popularity, possibly because of all the difficulties in breeding an outstanding specimen. Nevertheless such a mouse will always have its admirers.

A Himalayan mouse. Mouse breeders have not yet succeeded in producing Himalayans with dark points.

MARTEN SABLES

Generally speaking, the Marten Sable is a normal Sable whose belly is white instead of tan. In short, it is a Sable carrying the Chinchilla factor.

The N.M.C. Standard states: "Eye black. Top color shall be rich dark sepia from nose to tail, shading off to a paler color on lower jaws, sides and flanks, blending to be gradual; belly white, white ticking on flanks and rump to be considered an added beauty. Faults: light noses, blotches or streaks."

POINTS FOR MARTEN SABLES

Color	30
Level shading	10
Belly	10
Condition—not fat, short, sleek and glossy coat	15
Shape and carriage	10
Size	5
Ears—shape, size and position	5
Eyes—large, bold and prominent	5
Muzzle—long, strength carried out to end	5
Tail—long and uniform, no kinks	5
	100

Certificate 1958: V. Stephens, Esq.

It is difficult to give advice on this variety because no records are now available as to how they were originally bred; indeed this variety has only been rarely exhibited.

To build up a stud of Martens would probably require much time and experimentation. Initially normal Sables should be used, together with Silver Fox. The Silver Fox (preferably chocolate) is suggested instead of the Chinchilla because the Agouti coat pattern is not required. The standard also requests the long white guard hairs along the flanks, which are found only on the Fox. Since the chinchilla factor reduces yellow pigment to white, it appears that Marten Sables can be produced albeit with a great deal of effort.

THE SILVER FOX

The Silver Fox has proved to be exceedingly popular ever since its introduction to the fancy just three years after the Chinchilla. It has good size and type, fancier appeal and favorable specimens attain the highest honors. The Silver Fox is a variety that can be thoroughly recommended to the novice.

The N.M.C. Standard states: "Eye black. A Silver Fox shall be recognized in any of the following colors: black, blue, chocolate top color. Feet, sides and rump only to be ticked evenly with white hairs. Belly white."

POINTS FOR SILVER FOX

Top color	20
Belly	15
Ticking and feet	15
Condition—not fat, short, sleek and glossy coat	15
Shape and carriage	10
Size	5
Ears—shape, size and position	5
Eyes—large, bold and prominent	5
Muzzle—long, strength carried out to end	5
Tail—long and uniform, no kinks	5
	100

Certificate 1936: Dr. J.N. Pickard

Once it was discovered that the chinchilla factor cuts out yellow pigment, it was a simple matter to cross Chins to Black Tans and thus produce a mouse with a black top color but a pure white belly. Thus the Silver Fox was born. By mating to other colored Tans, different colored Foxes could be bred; however, the N.M.C. only accepts as standardized those Foxes with black, blue and chocolate top colors.

Although it should not be necessary, the fancier can produce his own strain of Foxes from Chins and Tans. The Tans should have good top color and strong tan because a richer tan when chinchillated appears whiter. Also, there should be an abundance of tan guard hairs along the flanks and over the rump, since they are an essential feature of the Silver Fox. The first generation will produce Agouti Tans that can either be mated together or again to Chinchillas. Subsequently, retain only those youngsters that have white bellies. Silver Fox will soon be produced although some might at the demarcation line show a slight tanning. The chin factor also has a slight reducing action on the top color, so it should not be expected that the top color will be of the same high quality as a Self or Tan. The Blue Fox is probably not so much affected in this way as are Blacks and Chocolates.

Although white guard hairs add much to the beauty of the Fox, odd white hairs on the back are a bad fault. The breeder should watch for them because mice with such odd hairs will be penalized by a discerning judge. Having been bred from Chins, the feet of the Silver Fox will unfortunately be all white, but this is a minor fault.

Once he has bred sufficient Foxes, the breeder should decide which of the three top colors he prefers and attempt to improve this often neglected feature which carries the most points in the standard.

THE SEAL POINT SIAMESE

The Seal Point Siamese is another variety which originally came from laboratory stock. Unlike so many varieties of fancy mice which can be compared to their equivalents in the rabbit or cavy, this mutation can be likened to the Siamese cat!

The standard for the Seal Point Siamese is as follows: "Eye: any color. Body color: medium beige. Shadings: gradually shaded over saddle and hind quarters, merging gradually with body color and being darkest at tail root as seen in the Siamese cat. The belly should be as near as possible in color and shadings. Points: Seal points, and shall be present in muzzle, ears, feet, tail and tail root. There should *not* be a definite or distinct line of demarcation but rather a toning in or merging with remainder of coat. At all times there should be a harmonious balance between body color, shadings and points. There should not be any blotches, streaks or white hairs."

POINTS FOR SEAL POINT SIAMESE
Color..15
Points...15
Shadings...15
Belly..10
Condition: not fat, short, sleek and glossy coat......10
Shape and carriage................................10
Size..5
Ears—shape, size and position.....................5
Eyes—large, bold and prominent....................5
Muzzle—long, strength carried out to end...........5
Tail—long and uniform, no kinks...................5
                                               100

Certificate 1969: Mrs. D. Cooper

The Seal Point Siamese gene is a completely new one to the fancy and the Himalayan variety has already been produced from it. It is a supremely attractive mouse and one that will be forever popular with exhibitors and breeders. The original stock had ruby eyes, although the present standard does not specifically require this anymore. Black-eyed Seal Point Siamese are easily produced by crossbreeding but it is felt that these mice do not match the red-eyed Seal Points in brightness of coloring and quality of shading.

In my opinion, the original ruby-eyed stock were the only true S.P.S. seen, much of the original beauty having been lost by indiscriminate crossbreeding. The problem is to discover a genetically suitable outcross, which was much needed to improve the size and type of the original stock that failed badly in this respect. As a suggestion, I believe Self Champagne would do least harm to the natural medium beige body color, without spoiling belly color either. When crossing S.P.S. to other varieties, many different colors arise; perhaps one worthy of mention is the Blue Point Siamese which is extremely pretty.

THE ASTREX

The mouse fancy boasts of just three coat mutations of which the oldest known is the Astrex.

The N.M.C. Standard is as follows: "An Astrex mouse shall have a coat as curly as possible, and like the Astrex rabbit, whiskers must be curly. The color may be that of any recognized variety."

POINTS FOR ASTREX

Curliness of coat	35
Color	20
Condition	10
Shape and carriage	10
Size	5
Ears—shape, size and position	5
Eyes—large, bold and prominent	5
Muzzle—long, strength carried out to end	5
Tail—long and uniform, no kinks	5
	100

Certificate 1936: A. Tuck, Esq.

The Astrex is an incredible mutation, for each hair of the mouse is altered to give the effect of curly waves throughout its coat. Even the whiskers must be curly! Unfortunately the waves or curls are not permanent. Up to the age of about eight weeks all is well but after that the coat seems to lose its curl and the adult Astrex looks very unattractive indeed. This is a great pity because many fanciers are consequently prevented from breeding and exhibiting this unusual mouse. The failing of the adult Astrex is well known to geneticists the world over. Perhaps the practical breeder could improve them by selection? It has been done before.

Size, type and general stamina are also failings of the Astrex but can be improved by direct crossing to normal fancy mice. As Astrex is recessive to the normal coat, the first generation will be normal but the second round should produce better Astrex without any loss of coat properties.

THE LONG HAIRED

The Long Haired is another laboratory mouse (the Astrex probably was as well) which has made great strides in the hands of fanciers. It is believed that the long haired mutation first occured in experiments against extreme climatic conditions.

The N.M.C. Standard states: "The long haired mouse shall have a coat as long as possible, combined with density and to be silky in texture. The color may be that of any recognized variety."

POINTS FOR LONG HAIRED

Coat—length, density and texture.................35
Color...20
Shape and carriage...............................10
Condition—not fat, clean and glossy coat..........10
Size..5
Ears—shape, size and position.....................5
Muzzle—long, strength carried out to end..........5
Tail—long and uniform, no kinks...................5
Eyes—large, bold and prominent....................5
                                                100

Certificate 1969: A.D. Jones, Esq.

A Long-Haired Mouse that was judged as the best in its class at the London and Southern Counties Mouse Club show.

The Long Haired suffers from a fault similar to that of the Astrex in that specimens appear to be better as youngsters than as adults. Baby Long Haired mice are like a beautiful bundle of fluff, but after about eight weeks of age their hair seems to stop growing. The mouse continues to fill out however and thus makes the hair appear to be shorter than it really is. Nevertheless, much improvement is being made and each new generation seems to have longer coats which last until adulthood.

The Long Haired is recognized in any standardized color but is most commonly seen in white and the best specimens have all been of this color. Other colors fairly easy to produce are B.E. Creams, Silvers, Champagnes and Argentes.

Type is the worst failing with this variety and the ears especially seem to be very small. Once this point has been improved and a better coat appears, the Long Haired will move to the top.

THE SATINS

This mouse is the most sensational mutation to be accepted by the N.M.C. It is one of the most beautiful of all mice, the satin coat giving even the most mediocre color a beautiful appearance.

The N.M.C. Standard states: "The Satin mouse shall have a high sheen coat resulting in an exquisite satin-like or metallic gloss. The color may be that of any recognized variety and should be as close as is possible to that variety having due regard to the effect of satinization. In particular: White shall be known as Ivory Satin."

The Satin is the latest laboratory mouse that has been recognized by the Executive Committee of the N.M.C. as having "fancier appeal." Although previously shown in the A.O.V. section, the Satin has in a short time become so popular that it has been granted a separate section of its own. The future of the Satin seems assured, and most of the popular varieties have now been satinized. This can be done simply by crossing Satin to a normal coated mouse of the required color. The first generation will all be Normals, but the second will produce both normals and Satins. The Satin babies can easily be distinguished and the Normals can then be culled.

Do not assume that all varieties will be popular when satinized since some varieties do benefit more than others. For example, Fawns, Reds and Argente Satins look especially attractive, but Blacks and Chocolates do not. In any case, the advent of the Satin mouse augurs well for the future of the mouse fancy; who knows what new and exciting mutations are still to come?

POINTS FOR SATIN

Satin coat	25
Color	25
Condition	15
Shape and carriage	10
Size	5
Ears	5
Eyes	5
Muzzle	5
Tail	5
	100

Certificate 1975: Mr. and Mrs. A. & G. Cooke

20: Building Up A Stud

The novice fanicer normally acquires a trio of his chosen variety from a reputable breeder, mates them, separates the does when pregnant and then asks himself, "what do I do next?" This is proverbial of the beginner. He has probably been to a successful fancier's mousery and seen box after box of top quality mice of all ages which comprise a stud. A stud such as this takes some time to perfect but should be the aim of every mouse fancier. The breeder is self-sufficient with such a stud of mice: he need not go outside his own mousery for stock, except in special circumstances if an outcross might be needed to improve a certain feature.

The novice, with only three mice, must wonder how he can buiild up his own stud to be consistently successful. Frankly speaking, he can't do this with just a trio. Even an experienced breeder would have difficulty building up a successful stud from one trio. It could be done but it would be far easier to start with say five does and one buck, or better still, with two trios that are not *closely* related (brothers and sisters). However, let us assume that our novice fancier has started with a trio. The first thing he must do is place each doe in a separate breeding box so that the mother and litter relationship can be ascertained. The buck should not be left alone. He may be required for stud purposes for another two months, so unless you can obtain more does from the original source, place an old waster pet shop mouse or two in with the buck to keep him company.

When each doe litters, the novice must decide just what he wishes to keep. It is best to ask an experienced fancier to sex the litters for you, but if this is not possible, the novice will have to try and do this himself, for he will not require many young bucks. There are two courses open. First, retain only does from the two litters; when mature (twelve weeks minimum) they can be mated back to the father. The two original does can be mated again to the buck in the meanwhile. Alternatively, a buck can be saved in each of the litters (as well as two or three does). These young bucks can either be mated to the adult does or to the young does of the other litter.

Perhaps the first system is best initially, but the original buck will not last forever, so it is as well to raise bucks from the second round of litters from the original does. There can be no hard and fast rules in breeding operations because it is no use keeping a buck or a doe merely for the sake of it. If it does not come up to standard, scrap it. Similarly, if the novice produces a buck that is better than the original sire, then discard his sire, for improvement has been made and he will no longer be needed. This may seem harsh, but it is the only way to build up a stud that will produce progressively better mice.

Whatever happens from the original trio, it will be seen that very close inbreeding will soon be taking place, because the breeder will not have the choice of matings that he would like. It is for this reason that it is preferable to commence with two trios. The novice should now return to the original source of supply and obtain a fresh stud buck and maybe a couple of does if the breeder can spare them. If the novice has noticed that the results of his own breeding have shown that a majority of his mice share a common fault (say small ears), then he should request a buck that excels in that particular feature.

It might be noticed that a certain strain sometimes suffers in one particular feature that has become an inherent factor within the family. For this reason many experienced fanciers obtain stock from two entirely different sources when taking up a new variety. This precaution particularly applies if there is no decent foundation stock available. By crossing the two trios together it is hoped that any inherent faults will be cancelled out, although obviously other faults may arise. Also size, type and general stamina should be increased from what is known as "hybrid vigor." This method should not be undertaken by the novice fancier until he gains more experience.

A selected outcross for any strain, perhaps a buck from another stud that excels in the point(s) required, can be experimented with. This outcross buck can be mated to a couple of does, the resultant litter being mated back into the strain. Take care to keep this bloodline entirely separate from the main stud so that if it is unsuccessful the entire experiment can be scrapped.

Many beginners inquire exactly how many mice constitute a stud. This is a difficult question to answer because it depends on many factors, such as quality of the stock, type of variety kept and the number of cages available. When initially building up a stud, it may be necessary to keep as many reasonably decent does as possible. As improvements are made, the standard of the stud becomes higher and thus many are discarded as being inferior.

It is argued that with some varieties, in particular the Dutch and Brokens, the breeder has to be a specialist in that variety and keep as many mice as possible. This is not always entirely correct, for if inferior marked specimens are retained, their faults will be bred into the strain. However, it is true to say that it is not necessary to keep as large a stud of Selfs, such as Creams or Champagnes, compared to Dutches to maintain consistent success. Probably the absolute minimum would be two good stud bucks and about ten adult breeding does, plus any good youngsters that are still growing. It is doubtful if more than say five bucks and thirty does are necessary, or even advisable. However many are kept, let quality rather than quantity be the rule. It is far better to have a few quality mice than an abundance of only average stock. If you have built up a stud of say fifty mice, but only five are good, then there is only one thing to do: discard the other forty-five.

Some beginners are advised to keep records of all their breeding operations on the grounds that the "faintest ink lasts longer than the strongest memory." This would be most commendable if it were only possible to devise a perfect system of record keeping. Mice cannot be ringed like rabbits or cage birds so there is now no way of identifying one mouse from another, especially if they are mice such as Whites which look very similar! However, the breeder should be able to identify his stud bucks which could be given numbers or letters on cards that can be moved with the buck from cage to cage. A similar card can be affixed to the cage of does he has serviced, together with the date of birth. This latter figure is important because the breeder can compare rate of growth of each litter and also see which contains a worthwhile specimen that is eligible for the under eight weeks class.

Apart from this, trying to keep records becomes an arduous task, with more time spent on writing out cards rather than tending to the needs of the livestock. Mice do not really live long enough for a pedigree to be made as in larger livestock, so the breeder should aim at consistent quality in his stud which could gain him an excellent reputation among fellow exhibitors.

21: Inbreeding

The term "inbreeding" suggests a pagan practice to many people, conjuring up all kinds of distasteful thoughts that are offered as reasons against its use. In short, to the layman it is a dirty word. However, all successful livestock breeders practice inbreeding to some extent. The farmer's prize herd of beefstock, Cruft's Supreme Champion, a winning strain of budgerigars or tropical fish are all the end product of inbreeding. The little mouse is no different, so if the fancier wishes to be consistently successful he must practice the art and science (for it is both) of inbreeding.

Let's at first define inbreeding and its alternative, outcrossing. Inbreeding means "breeding in" the features of the strain so that all succeeding generations have these features; outcrossing is the mating together of two totally unrelated specimens. It can be seen immediately that the breeder will be reasonably certain of what the progeny will look like from inbreeding, but it is anyone's guess what color or form outcrossing will produce.

Inbreeding can be harmful if carried out incorrectly and will produce weak, undersized stock. However, this is probably due to using poor stock in the first place. Inbreeding does not put anything into a family strain that is not already there, though it does accentuate the faults as well as the good points of the bloodline, and this is where the skill of the breeder is tested.

Use only the very best specimens at any time. If a mouse is lacking in stamina, then no matter how good he is on other points, such as color, markings, etc., he should not be used. The failure of some fanciers to adhere to this policy produces the poor results which have given inbreeding a bad name. Another common mistake of fanciers is to breed every possible doe, no matter how poor, to the best stud buck, in the hope that the youngsters will be up to standard. It cannot be stressed too strongly that the sexes have an equal influence on the progeny, so the doe must be of the highest standard.

Obviously the buck is of the utmost importance because he serves so many different does, and so his likeness will be firmly stamped on future generations. A good way to obtain a first class stud buck is to let two or three does raise bucks only. Reduce the litter by keeping only the biggest bucks, and as they grow older keep reducing since defects become apparent only when one or two are left. These bucks should remain with their mothers until they are ready for stud purposes. They will probably mate up with the adult does, but this will not matter. A fine, hefty masculine stud should be the result, provided it has been fed properly.

Although inbreeding has much to commend it, close inbreeding is neither necessary nor desirable; brother to sister, for example, is not a worthwhile mating. Most top breeders practice a system of line breeding whereby two or three separate lines are maintained, each headed by its own stud buck. These lines will all be of exactly the same blood and can be crossed to each other as necessary. In this way the breeder can carry on for many years without resorting to fresh blood, yet general health is always maintained.

Critics of inbreeding should remember the Golden Hamster. Many millions of this small animal have been produced and are kept in homes and laboratories around the world. They make an excellent exhibition animal of the best possible health, size and stamina. Every known hamster originates from just one female and her litter that was unearthed in the wild!

"Like begets like" is an old adage that every breeder of livestock would do well to keep in his mind at all times. If only the best are used it follows that only the best will be bred. This is so obvious that it seems too simple to be true yet even so, the breeder must be on his guard and study his stock carefully. Once a good stud has been built up the fancier cannot rest on his laurels. He cannot stand still either; he must continually progress, or he will go backwards.

To sum up, inbreeding is not harmful if correctly done. This means selecting only the best with each succeeding generation. Success lies in the hands of the breeder, who must use his own skill to improve his strain.

22: Genetics

A book such as this is not concerned with the splitting of cells, chromosomes and the big 'A's and little 'a's of genetic formulas. In any case, 99% of mouse fanciers are practical breeders who do not necessarily understand genetics, but who do know how to breed winners!

Although a detailed understanding of genetics is not necessary to build up a top class stud of fancy mice, a little knowledge is not always a dangerous thing. A basic knowledge of the fundamentals of color inheritance would help every fancier towards his goal, since it would cut out trial and error methods and could also provide short cuts. Therefore, every fancier should try to grasp at least the fundamentals. The section on each individual variety in this book contains methods to produce or improve certain colors. Most of these suggestions have been tried and tested over the years and hopefully will prove to be of help to you.

For genetic purposes the mouse is divided into four groups. Thus, there is the black group consisting of the Self Black, Blue, Dove and Silver. The Chocolate group includes the Self Chocolate and Champagne. The yellow group consists of Reds, Fawns and Sables. The Agouti group includes the Agouti, Cinnamon, Chinchilla, Argente and Argente Creme.

Mention should be made of the terms dominant and recessive. When two different colors are mated one may be dominant to the other. Thus Black is dominant to Chocolate, and when these two colors are crossed the resultant litter will be all Blacks. However, they will carry the factor for producing Chocolates (the recessive color) and will produce a percentage of Chocolates in the next generation. Generally speaking, mice of the yellow group are the most dominant, and this includes tan belly colors. Then comes the Agouti which is dominant to Self, and Self which is dominant to Pied. Normal coat is dominant to Astrex, Long Haired or Satin coat. Black eye is dominant to pink eye.

Probably the most important factor in color inheritance of the mouse is the pink-eye dilution action. For example, this turns Black to Dove, Chocolate to Champagne and Agouti to Argente. This factor creates a whole new range of coat colors which are extremely attractive and have become successful on the show bench.

The Chinchilla, by its unique action of reducing yellow pigment to white, has also played a tremendous part in producing new colors. There are other genes not classified in the above of course, such as the Seal Point Siamese and the Himalayan. In fact, the classification of genetic formulas for mice is unending.

23: Experimental Breeding

Many fanciers gain immense pleasure out of keeping fancy mice without ever winning big prizes. These fanciers may attend shows only occasionally, exhibit standardized varieties even less often and never aspire to achieve championships, Best in Shows or N.M.C. trophies.

The great interest of these fanciers is in experimental breeding. Trying to breed to perfection a variety that is already popular is to them purely academic, uninteresting and unexciting. However, breeding something new that has never been dreamt of before is a challenge that some cannot resist. The possible color and coat mutations of the fancy mouse are limitless, so there is always the chance of someone making a name for himself by producing a new variety. This is not to say that the experimental breeders of the fancy are glory hunters (they are certainly not pot hunters), for they also take an interest in the neglected varieties or those that have become lost to the fancy. Thus experimentalists are always trying, one way or another, to popularize or re-introduce such varieties as the B.E. Whites, Variegated, Marten Sables, Silver Fawns, Browns and Pearls. Such efforts deserve much praise, for there can never be too many varieties of fancy mice.

The ultimate aim of the experimental breeder is to produce a new variety and have it recognized by the

N.M.C. It is relatively easy to produce some sort of color that is not already standardized, but it is not quite that simple. The Executive Committee of the N.M.C. requires a possible new variety to be distinctive from existing varieties and to have "fancier appeal." It would be a waste of time to submit a new variety for approval if its appearance were similar to an existing breed. The new variety must be attractive and have what is termed "fancier appeal," since the Committee must be convinced that fanciers would be sufficiently interested to take up the new variety and to breed and exhibit it at shows.

The N.M.C. rule states: "the Executive may grant a New Variety Certificate to any member who introduces a new variety of mouse. Before making an award the member must have exhibited a team of at least three mice of the proposed new variety at a show held under club patronage. A provisional standard will be held for two years, after which time a Certificate shall be considered by the Executive for final approval."

Some unstandardized varieties come near to being recognized, and breeders often produce them through experimental color breeding. The Blue Agouti and Blue Sable are old favorites. They are produced by crossings to Self Blue and Blue Tan, respectively, and produce the new varieties as a result of the blue dilution factor. The Lilac was once standardized in Selfs and Fox. It is easy to produce by crossing Blue to Chocolate and is rather similar in color to Dove. However, it was never popular and was dropped from the standards.

The silvered group provides many different color forms, all showing silvering. Most common are Silver Blue and Silver Chocolate and these are sometimes exhibited as light Silver Grays and Silver Browns respectively. A good judge would not let them pass, however. During experiments with the silvered group other attractive colors crop up such as Silvered Sables, Silvered

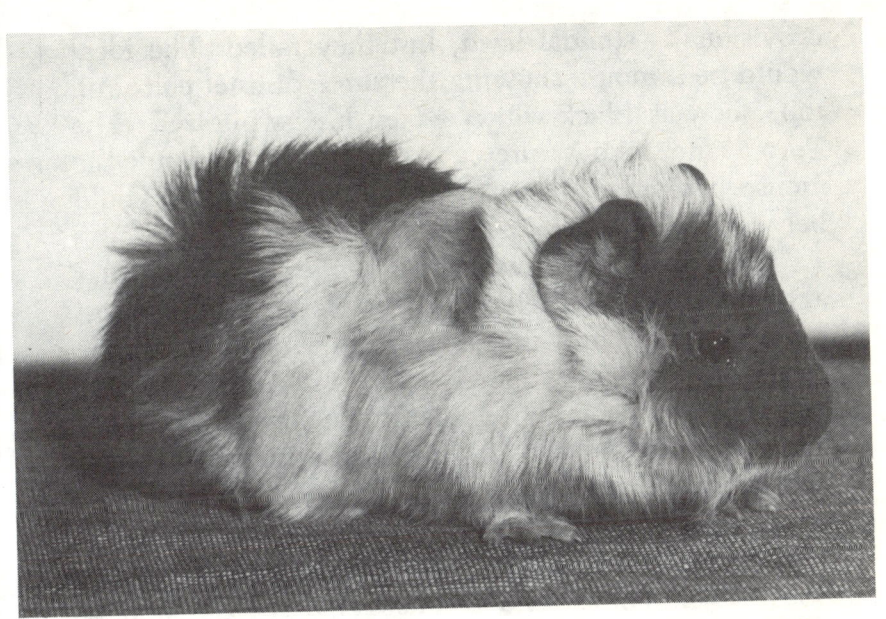

The tri-colored mouse is still an unrealized feat in mice breeding. This Tortoiseshell and White cavy mutation would be an ideal model. Photo by M.F. Roberts.

Cinnamons and Pearls and anything but gray or black tipping. The silvered group and the Chinchilla are the breeds most often used in experiments.

Laboratories also house exciting new mutations that could be of use to the fancy. Some decry the use of laboratory stock, yet successful varieties such as the Chinchilla, Rump White, Long Haired and Satin originaly came from laboratories. Possible new varieties from this source could include a red coated mouse and a white banded or belted mouse (similar to the banded hamster).

Without doubt the most prized achievement in experimental breeding would be to introduce a genuine tricolored mouse, the object of every mouse fancier since the inception of the club. There have been many attempts in the past, and many so called tricolors were

213

provisionally standardized, but they failed. The ideal would be a mouse showing the three distinct colors on top, such as black-white-red or blue-white-red. The Tortoiseshell and White cavy mutation would suit the mouse perfectly. What an attractive animal it would be!

Also permissible would be a mutation somewhat akin to the Tortoiseshell cat, although this gene is sex influenced in that only one of the sexes actually shows the gene while the other merely carries it. Unfortunately, there does not seem to be a scientific method for producing a tricolored mouse; we must wait until such a mutation occurs by chance.

The mouse is one of the best animals to use for the fancier interested in studying color inheritance. Mutations are numerous and results are quickly produced with such a short gestation period and rapid sexual maturity. Even the experimentalist should start with good mice, sound in size, type and stamina. For if he were fortunate enough to produce a new variety, it would be a pity if the mouse lacked in the points essential to all exhibition mice.

24: Fancy Rats

A book such as this would perhaps not be complete without a chapter about the larger cousin of the mouse, the fancy rat. Up to the 1930's fancy rats were catered for by the N.M.C., which was then known as the National Mouse and Rat Club. Popularity of the exhiition rat waned, however, and although there have been several revivals since then, the rat will probably never return to prominence. Most of the old varieties have been lost, although the raw material is still available in pet shops and laboratories. It must also be remembered that our forefathers began with stock trapped from the wild! This abhorence of the wild rat has perhaps prevented the domesticated fancy varieties from becoming popular as exhibition animals. However, rats make very good show animals, breed easily, cost little to feed, are hygenic and are available in many attractive colors.

The genus *Rattus* is extremely large, but for our purposes can be divided into two groups that can be domesticated: the black rat, *Rattus rattus*, and the brown rat, *Rattus norvegicus*. Both types have been exhibited in the past in various forms and colors, but the brown rat has proven to be the most popular and can be found in a greater variety of colors and markings. Hybridization between the two species has never been recorded. Fancy rats can be exhibited in much the same way as mice, except that the Maxey patterned show cage must obviously be larger. A base of nine inches x nine inches would be ideal.

The old standard of excellence for the fancy rat as laid down by the N.M. and R.C. was as follows: "The fancy rat should be of good size, long and racy in shape, arched over loin, plump and firm with clean long head, not too fine or pointed at the nose. The eyes should be bold and prominent and of good size. Ears, feet and tail should be free from warts or roughness. The coat should be close, soft and glossy, sleek to the touch and not too long. In bucks the coat is apt to be somewhat harder and longer than in does. The tail should be well set on, thickish at the butt end, clean and tapering to a fine point, the length being equal to the body from end of muzzle to root of tail. The ears should be of good size, tulip shaped and not set too close

A Silver Fawn rat. Fanciers prefer those colors that are distinct from the agouti color of the wild rat.

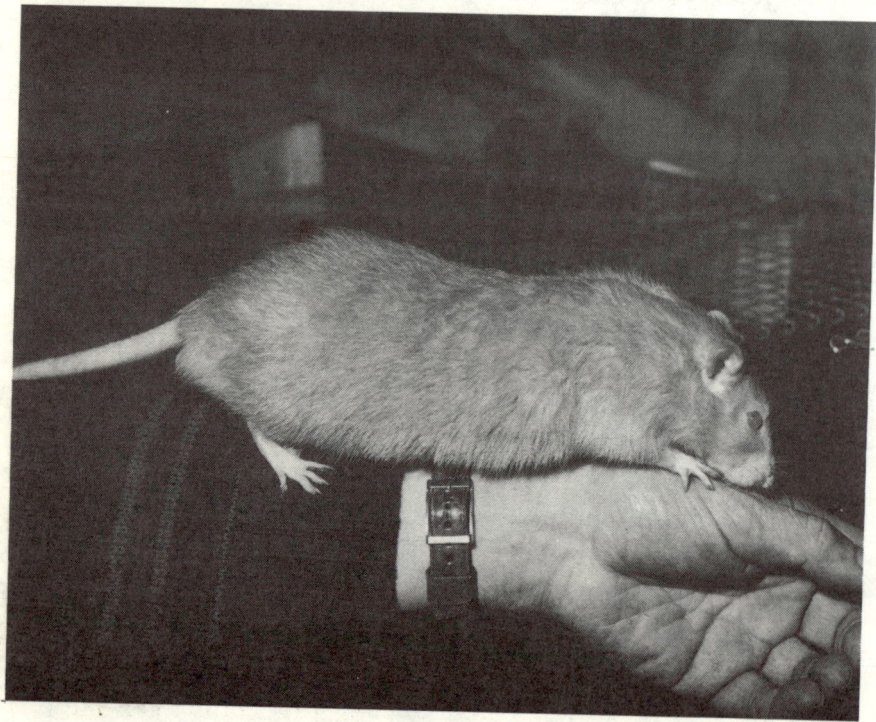

A young Capped Rat. Color is confined to the head area only; it does not appear on the ears or body.

together. In Selfs, the feet, ears and tail should be slightly covered with fur as nearly as possible the color of the body. The rat should be perfectly tractable, free from any vice and not subject to fits or other ailments. Kinked tails to be penalized 20 points."

Although the fancy varieties of the rat are nowhere near as numerous as the mouse, there are still some attractive colors. In Selfs there are Whites, Blacks, Blues, Chocolates, Creams, Fawns, Champagnes and Doves. There are also Agoutis, although these are not so popular, being similar to the wild type.

One of the most successful breeds has always been the Japanese hooded, which has a colored head and dorsal stripe on a white body. Similar to the Japanese is the Capped or hooded where only the head is colored, but not beyond the ears. These two varieties come in various

217

colors, with pink or black eyes, as does the Irish, which has four white feet and a white triangle on the chest between the front legs. The Berkshire has a colored top with a completely white belly; its feet and tail are white, with a small spot between the ears. A popular variety today is the Argente. It has been called Silver Fawn, but is actually an Agouti carrying the pink-eyed dilution factor. It seems, from old records, that Silver Grays have been exhibited, but they were most probably poor Blacks, showing white hairs.

The colors in the fancy rat have not been as cultivated as the mouse; in particular a color such as black appears slate-gray. A washing (as described in the

A new variety of rat for which breed standards are not yet established.

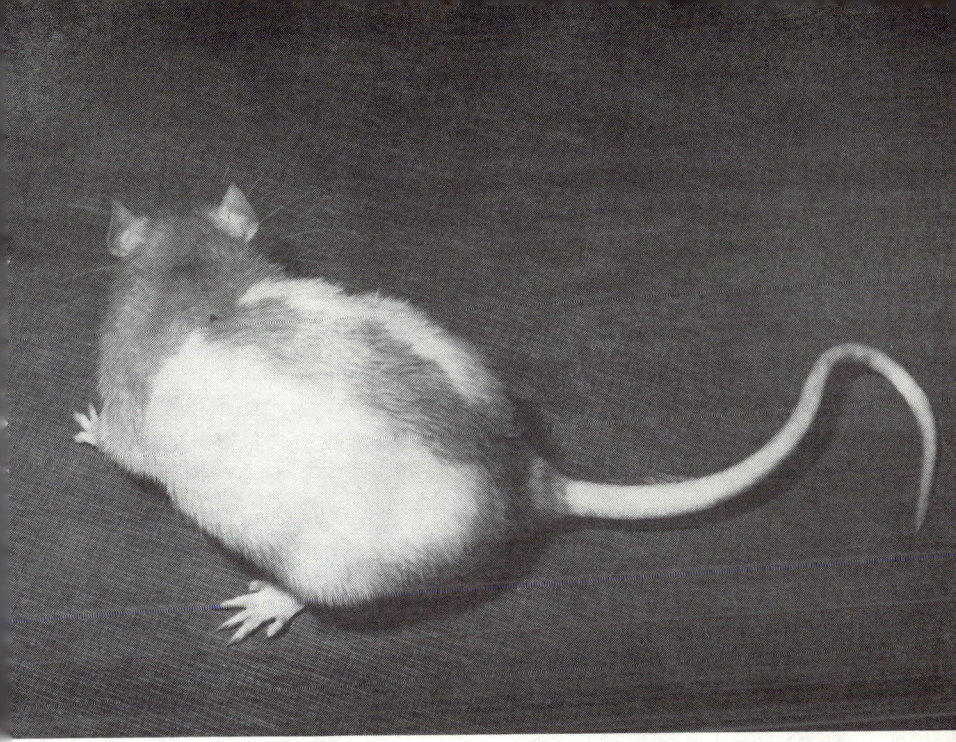

A young Japanese Hooded rat with its dorsal marking shown.

chapter on pink-eyed white mice) would be most beneficial for exhibition rats, making their coats both cleaner and softer.

Feeding presents few problems, being basically the same as for mice. In addition to commercial feeds obtainable at any pet store, household scraps together with fresh greens can be given. Rats also relish a meaty bone occasionally. Water should be given, preferably in bottles obtainable from pet shops. Rats obviously require larger accommodations than mice. A cage two foot square would be sufficient for two to six occupants. Wood is the most suitable material, although it may be a wise precaution to cover the inside of the roof and sides with wire to prevent gnawing. A wire-covered door in the style of a rabbit hutch would be ideal so that the owner could see his pets, provided the cage is not facing a direct draft. A shelf can be fixed along the back of the cage to afford exercise for the inmates. Ladders, ropes

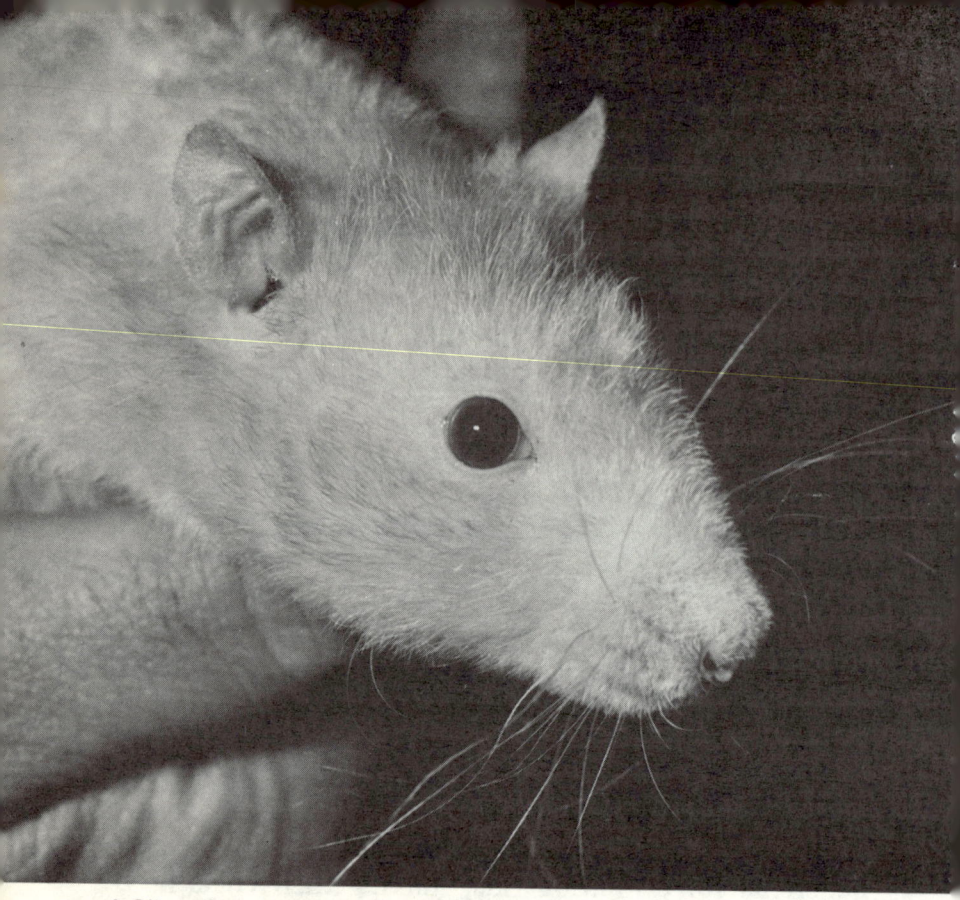

A Silver Fawn (curly-coated) rat. Note the curly whiskers.

or wheels can also be used to keep the rats occupied. The floor of the cage should be strewn with about a one-half inch layer of sawdust, which should be scraped out and renewed when it becomes damp and soiled. Sweet fresh hay is the best form of bedding and will also be eaten by the rats.

Rats are gregarious animals and will soon lose condition if kept alone. They should be handled as much as possible, whether they are pets or exhibition animals. The greatest advantage rats have over mice is that male rats can be housed together without fighting. However be careful not to introduce a strange rat, of either sex, into a cage already occupied, because the stranger will not be accepted.

The gestation period of the rat is about twenty-eight days. The young, of which there may be as many as sixteen, are born naked, blind and deaf. They are fully furred at twelve days and open their eyes around fifteen days. They begin to eat solid foods at this age, starting with any soft foods that the doe brings into the nest, and eat freely from the food dish at three weeks.

Rats are sexually mature at 12 weeks and may even mate earlier than this. It is preferable to wait until about 16 weeks so that the doe is strong enough to raise the litter. Culling is not as necessary to the maximum growth as it is with mice, although it is advised so that the breeder is not burdened with unwanted stock. The male should be removed from the breeding cage or matings will occur almost immediately after birth. Two does will successfully raise their young together.

The fancy rat is not prone to many diseases if properly housed and fed. Most ailments are identical to those of the mouse (see chapter ten) and a rat with asthma or cancerous tumors should be painlessly destroyed. A complaint common about the rat comes in the form of pimply ears and tail, which can be easily cured in a few days by applying a mixture of olive oil and flowers of sulphur.

The fancy rat can be recommended as an interesting, intelligent pet. It, too, has a future as an exhibition animal, provided breeders are sufficiently interested in this side of the hobby.

The late Walter Maxey wrote: "The rat is a most intelligent and affectionate animal, and even those taken in the wild state can be quickly made to respond to a little kindness, and once gaining his confidence he will become tame and gentle." What better testimonial could a rat have?

INDEX

Page numbers printed in bold race refer to photographs.

A
Abbreviations and terms, 80-1
Agouti Dutch mouse, **178**
Ailments, 69-70
Any Other Variety (AOV), 166-201
Aquarium, 14, **16**
Agouti and Cinnamon Tan mouse, 134-5
Argente Creme mouse, **113**, 186-7
Argente mouse, **57**
Argentes, 182-5
Asthma, 70
Astrex, 197-8
Awards, 75

B
Bedding, **30**, 42-3, **31**
Black, 106-9, **107**
Black-Eyed Cream, **102**, **187**
Black-Eyed Whites, 106
Black Fox, **188**
Black Tan mouse, **109**, 112
Black Tans, 130-1
Blue, 110
Blue Fox mouse, **169**
Blue Tan mouse, **108**
Blue Tans, 131, 133
Blue-Eyed Cream mouse, **187**
Breeding, 55, 58, 63, 66
Breeding boxes, 38-9, **44**, **52**, **60**
Broken mouse, **48**
Broken-Marked mouse, **151**
Brokens, 150-4

C
Cages, **15**, **18**, **19**
Capped rat, 217
Champagne, 114

Champagne Tan, 135-6
Championship show, 75
Chinchilla, **165**, **168**, **172**, **174**, 174-7
Chocolate, 110-11
Chocolate Tan, 131
Chocolate White Rump mouse, **125**
Cinnamon mouse, **173**
Classes, 78-9, 99
Conditioning food, 87-8
Cod liver oil, **86**
Cooke, Tony, **95**
Cream, **49**, 112-4
Culling, 63, 66

D
Diarrhea, 69
Doves, 118-9
Dutch, **15**, **142**, 142-7
Dutch-Marked mouse, **177**

E
Entry forms, 81
Evens, 154-7
Exercise wheel, 19, **136**
Experimental breeding, 211-4

F
Fancy rats, 215-21
Feeding, 46, 50-1, 53-4
Female mouse, **62**, **66**
Fawn, 124-6
Fawn Satin mouse, **121**
Fostering, 67-8

G
Genetics, 209-10

222

Golden Agouti mouse, **60**
Golden Agoutis and Cinnamons, 166-71
Gray mouse, **156**
Grooming, 85

H
Hagen Habitat, **16**
Hartley, Jack, **107**
Heating, 28-9
Himalayan, **41**, 159-62, **162, 164, 192**
Holding, **36, 37, 90, 153**
Holland, Dan, **91**
Housing, 26-9

I
Inbreeding, 206-8
Ivory Satin mouse, **97**

J
Japanese Hooded rat, **219**
Judges, **22, 33, 82, 84, 89, 90, 91, 94, 107, 117**

L
Lighting, 28
Long-haired, **8, 45**, 198-200, **199**

M
Male mouse, **59, 66**
Marked, 138-9, 142-65
Marten Sable, 192-3
Maxey cages, **43**, 72, **73, 74**, 87, 88, **116**
Maxey Walter, 9, **11**
Mendel Gold Cup, 76
Mus musculus, 9, 10

N
National Mouse Club (N.M.C.), 9
Newly born mice, 62, **63, 64, 133**

Nylabone, 20

O
Open show, 73, 75

P
Parasite, 70
Pearl mouse, **101, 104**
Pearls, 182
P.E. Whites, 103-6
Pink-Eyed Self Silver mouse, **45**
Plastic cage, **15**
Points for:
    Agoutis and Cinnamons, 168
    Argente Creme, 186
    Argentes, 183
    Astrex, 197
    Brokens, 150
    Chinchillas, 175
    Dutch-Marked, 100
    Even-Marked, 155
    Himalayans, 159
    Long-Haired, 198
    Marten Sables, 193
    Rump Whites, 163
    Sables, 189
    Satin, 201
    Seal Point Siamese, 196
    Self Varieties, 101
    Silver Fox, 194
    Silver Grays, Browns and Fawns, 178
    Tan Varieties, 127
    Variegated, 158
Purchasing mice, 21-4

R
Racks, **27**, 30-5, *34, 39, 44*
Rattus norvegicus, 215
Rattus rattus, 215
Rex mouse, **48**
Rump White, **162**

S
Sables, **120**, 187-91
Satins, **61**, 200-1
Seal Point Siamese, **128, 162,** 195-7
Seeds, **47, 56**
Self Champagne, **125, 161**
Self Cream, **41**
Self Doves, **100**
Self Red, **117, 176**
Selfs, 100-26
Shows, **23, 43, 94, 167**
Show preparation, 85-92
Showing, 72-84
Silver, 116-8
Silver Agouti, 171-5
Silver and Dove Tans, 134
Silver Fawn rat, **220**
Silver Fox, 193-5
Silver Gray, **185**
Silver Gray, Fawn or Brown, 178-80
Silver Gray and Pearl Tans, 135

Silver Tan mouse, **105**
Smith, E.N., **117**
Standard of Excellence, 98
Stewarding, 93-6
Strutt, Jon, **33**
Stud, Building-up a, 202-5

T
Table show, 73
Tans, 127-35
Tortoiseshell and White cavy, **213**
Travelling box, **53, 74**
Tumors, 70

V
Variegated, 157-8
Ventilation, 28

W
Waterer, gravity-fed, **51**
White Rump mouse, **89**
Wild mouse, **157**